IRELAND: THE EMIGRANT NURSERY AND THE WORLD ECONOMY

UNDERCURRENTS

Published titles in the series

Facing the Unemployment Crisis in Ireland by Kieran Kennedy
Divorce in Ireland: Who Should Bear the Cost? by Peter Ward
Crime and Crisis in Ireland: Justice by Illusion? by Caroline Fennell
The Hidden Tradition: Feminism, Women and Nationalism in Ireland
by Carol Coulter
Managing the EU Structural Funds by Alan Matthews
*Diverse Communities: The Evolution of Lesbian and Gay Politics in
Ireland* by Kieran Rose
*Democracy Blindfolded: The Case for a Freedom of Information Act in
Ireland* by Patrick Smyth and Ronan Brady

Forthcoming titles will include

Susan Ryan-Sheridan on new reproductive technologies in Ireland

UNDERCURRENTS Series Editor Fintan O'Toole

Ireland: The Emigrant Nursery and the World Economy

JIM MAC LAUGHLIN

CORK UNIVERSITY PRESS

First published in 1994 by
Cork University Press
University College
Cork
Ireland

British Library Cataloguing in Publication Data

A CIP catalogue record for this book is available from the British Library

ISBN 1 85918 028 0

Typeset in Ireland by Seton Music Graphics Ltd, Co. Cork
Printed in Ireland by ColourBooks, Baldoyle, Co. Dublin

CONTENTS

INTRODUCTION

Irish emigration, an important *diagnostic* feature of Irish society and indeed the world economy, has attracted surprisingly little theoretical attention, although it has attracted the attention of modernisation theorists, historians and demographers.[1] Most recent accounts are simply atheoretical descriptions of its impact at home and its contribution to the Irish 'diaspora' abroad. Framed in the narrow logic of cost – benefit analysis, these descriptions often reduce emigration to simple economic causes and consequences or explain it away in terms of the 'push' and 'pull' factors operating between Ireland and the international economy. Moreover, it could be argued that we are better informed about the emigration of nineteenth-century farm labourers and the social status of the Irish in Victorian Britain than we are about 'new wave' emigration of school-leavers since the '80s. This concentration on the past and the comparative neglect of contemporary aspects of Irish emigration is not simply a reflection of the extent to which historians have monopolised the study of Irish emigration; it also reflects a widespread tendency to treat emigration as a *cultural* and *historical* tradition with contemporary ramifications. This has contributed to the naturalisation and sanitisation of emigration in recent years.

This study focuses on historical and contemporary aspects of Irish emigration. It suggests that emigration is an intrinsically social geographical phenomenon because it is linked to processes of core formation and peripheralisation on national and international scales. Emigration clearly also has social geographical causes and consequences. It has, for example, been responsible for the construction and destruction of places and lived environments. This study, however, seriously challenges purely *geographical* and *behavioural* explanations which have traced emigration to the social psychological attributes and attitudes of Irish young adults, or explained it away in terms of Ireland's geographical location relative to Europe and the world economy. Adopting the logic of world-systems theory it argues that persistent and widespread Irish emigration is indicative of the peripheral *status*, and not just the peripheral *location* of the Irish state in the world economy. Analysing a number of major surveys of recent Irish emigration, this study suggests that Ireland still operates as an emigrant nursery today, and that it is much too premature to talk of the modernisation or gentrification of Irish emigration.

The analysis proceeds as follows. Chapter one traces the emergence of Ireland as an 'emigrant nursery' and the relationship between emigration, class formation and core formation in the nineteenth and early-twentieth century. Chapter two briefly examines official attitudes to Irish emigration in the late-nineteenth and early-twentieth century and contrasts historic with contemporary attitudes to emigration. Chapter three discusses the social composition, destinations and the political and economic functions of Irish emigration between the foundation of the state and the 1960s. Chapter four argues that the current naturalisation and sanitisation of Irish emigration can be traced to behavioural and geographical explanations of migration and emigration in the 1960s. This chapter also offers an alternative explanation which focuses on the structural roots of emigration and Ireland's role in the international division of labour. The final chapter provides a detailed critical analysis of 'new-wave' emigration which suggests that recent Irish emigrants have not been climbing social ladders in sufficiently large numbers to merit a categorisation of recent Irish emigration as a fundamentally new development which has allowed 'the new Irish emigrants' to satisfy their social and economic aspirations abroad.

1. EMIGRATION AND CAPITALIST DEVELOPMENT IN NINETEENTH-CENTURY IRELAND

THE EMERGENCE OF THE EMIGRANT NURSERY

Emigration has been inextricably linked to the process of class formation and capitalist development in Ireland since at least the eighteenth century. Many historians have commented on the fact that the volume of Irish emigration in the nineteenth century was such that surplus labour, not just surplus value, constituted the major export of rural and urban Ireland. Irish emigration has variously been attributed to the disintegration of Irish peasant society, the modernisation of Irish agriculture and the development of bourgeois values and aspirations in rural Ireland. Lyons interpreted the head-long exodus of one million people from Ireland between 1845 and 1851 as 'the instinctive reaction of a panic-stricken people to the spectacle of their traditional way of life breaking into pieces before their very eyes'.[2] In the midlands and south-east of Ireland, emigration was also a rational response to the commercialisation of Irish agriculture and to structural transformations in the world economy which fuelled demand for migrant labour and emigrants alike. Indeed *modern* Irish emigration dates from the early-nineteenth century when large tracts of the country were transformed from relatively self-contained rural communities into emigrant nurseries which supplied cheap and adaptable labour for the modern world system.[3] Kirby A. Miller has argued that in the middle of the century, Ireland:

> was little more than an inferior appendage of British capitalism and imperialism . . . This was the crucial,

colonial context in which Irish modernization occurred, determined and distorted by the priorities and tastes of the sister island. Consequently, Ireland's economic development, its further integration into world capitalism, was highly uneven, specialized, and dependent. . . . In fact, Ireland's social adjustments to the exigencies of colonialism and world capitalism – adjustments dictated by external pressures and internal inequities – mandated massive, sustained emigration. Put bluntly, *emigration became a societal imperative of post-Famine Ireland*: in reality less a choice than a vital necessity both to secure the livelihoods of nearly all who left and most who stayed and to ensure the relative stability of *a fundamentally 'sick' society which offered its lower classes and most of its young people 'equal opportunities' only for aimless poverty at home or menial labour and slum tenements abroad.* (Emphasis added)[4]

An estimated 7 million people left Ireland for North America alone, between the beginning of the seventeenth century to the foundation of the Irish state. Between 1851 and 1921, just under 4.5 million Irish emigrants settled in North America, Australia and New Zealand. An estimated 4 million Irish moved to the United States alone between 1846 and 1925. By way of comparison, the corresponding figures for the number of emigrants from the United Kingdom, Germany and Scandinavia who moved to the United States at this time were 3.97, 5.41 and 7.6 million respectively. Similarly, an estimated 3.5 million Russians, two-thirds of them Jews, and 12.23 million Italians settled in the United States between the mid-1860s and the mid-1920s.[5] Miller has argued that this vast flow:

was at once a barometer of the social and economic changes taking place on both sides of the Atlantic and itself *a major determinant of the modern shapes of North*

American and Irish societies. In spite of the diminutive size of their homeland, the Irish played an important role in the commercial and industrial revolutions that transformed the North Atlantic world. (Emphasis added)[6]

Table 1.1: Population of Ireland between 1841 and 1911.

Year	Population (000s)	Year	Population (000s)
1841	6,529	1881	3,870
1851	5,112	1891	3,469
1861	4,402	1901	3,222
1871	4,053	1911	3,140

Source: *The Social and Economic Implications of Emigration* (National Economic and Social Council, March, 1991), p. 48.

Emigration on this scale certainly placed Ireland among the leading European exporters of labour between the mid-nineteenth and the early-twentieth century. Given the size of the country, and the intensity of the exodus, Irish emigration was at least on a par with some of the greatest migratory movements in modern history, including the shipment of approximately 9.5 million live African slaves to the Americas between 1450 and 1871.[7] Given the fact that the Irish not only gravitated to the urban centres of the east coast of North America but also played a significant role in clearing native Americans from the interior, they were among the chief benefactors of white colonial and capitalist expansion in North America. Irish involvement in bitter 'race wars' against native and black Americans is a forgotten chapter in current debates on Ireland's internationalist and anti-colonial legacy.

Given its scale and social composition, Irish emigration clearly fulfilled a number of important functions within Ireland and the world economy. Firstly, it contributed to the Anglicisation of Ireland by transforming the geolinguistic map of Ireland and greatly reducing the number of Irish speakers in the country. Secondly, it facilitated the commercialisation of Irish agriculture and made Ireland a major emigrant nursery in the world economy. Thirdly, it intensified the eastward drift of political power in Ireland and exacerbated its socio-spatial concentration in the rich agricultural heartlands and in the east of the country. Fourthly, emigration, particularly after the Famine, revealed the extent to which socio-economic life in Ireland was determined by forces operating at the level of the international and not just the national economy. Fifthly, together with the Great Famine – and other famines that preceded the 'Hungry Forties' – emigration fundamentally altered power relations in Ireland by removing large numbers of young adults from the land just when they came of political age. Finally, as the century progressed, emigration contributed to the abatement of social tensions on family farms in the rich agricultural regions and in peripheral areas in the west and north-west of the country. The large-scale removal abroad of Mother Ireland's 'surplus' sons and daughters contributed to the reduction of class conflict and fostered political stability in an otherwise volatile and class-structured society. In so doing it barred any possibility of a fundamentally social or political revolution in nineteenth-century Ireland.

Several other factors contributed to the transformation of Ireland into a major emigrant nursery in the latter half of the nineteenth century. Firstly, Ireland's entry into a free-trade capitalist system dominated by England and the United States hastened the de-industrialisation of the south of the country through the emigration of large numbers of agricultural labourers, artisans and craft-workers. Secondly, international competition dictated the further modernisation of agriculture in the south of Ireland and the concentration of industry in and around Belfast city and its environs. However, the progressive diversification of the north-east's industrial base through the addition of shipbuilding, engineering and related industries did not mean that all of those formerly employed in the countryside were now absorbed into Belfast's expanding but deeply sectarian labour market. It was soon apparent that the city was never meant to be a haven for poor Catholics fleeing poverty and landlessness in the south of Ireland. In 1851 Belfast's population of 87,000 inhabitants was a mere third of Dublin's. By 1911 the population of the city exceeded that of Dublin by more than 64,000 inhabitants. More significant than this absolute growth were the marked differentials in the growth rates of the Catholic and Protestant populations in the city. Between 1861 and 1911 the Protestant population of Belfast quadrupled to 293,704 while the Catholic population increased by 125 per cent to just 93,243 inhabitants.[8]

Thirdly, the heightened commercialisation and specialisation of Irish agriculture transformed Ireland into an emigrant nursery by exposing the cottier class, middling tenants and large farmers to the perils of redundancy and international competition throughout the second half of the nineteenth and the opening decades of the twentieth century.[9] It also exposed them to crop failures and declining prices and caused the surplus sons, and particularly the surplus daughters, of poor families to be jettisoned onto the emigrant trail at an early age. The commercialisation of farming formalised and revolutionised social relations within the family and gradually paved the way for the destruction of the extended family. This obliged large and small farmers alike to adopt marriage and inheritance patterns which caused large numbers of the sons and daughters of rural Ireland to be banished from 'Mother Ireland'. As the century progressed, many of those who would formerly have been supported within the family or within the extended family were forced into seasonal or permanent emigration at a comparatively early age. Many more, particularly young children, were literally sold at 'hiring fairs' in order that poor rural and working-class families might supplement meagre cash incomes in areas where opportunities for adults to do this were very few. A final factor which contributed to the transformation of Ireland into an emigrant nursery was the fact that changing market conditions in the world economy caused pronounced shifts from tillage to cattle production in Ireland and forced more and more young adults to leave for destinations which led to the outer limits of the expanding capitalist system. Just as today the Irish have been responsible for 'filling gaps' in the international labour market, in the nineteenth century they often literally 'peopled' the frontiers of the world economy. This was particularly the case in North America, Australia and south Africa.

EMIGRATION, CAPITAL ACCUMULATION AND BOURGEOIS HEGEMONY IN RURAL IRELAND

Marx was among the first to emphasise the links between capital accumulation, class configuration, core formation and the global dispersal of the rural poor from nineteenth-century Ireland.[10] In particular he argued that the global division of labour which emerged in the latter half of the century favoured the core areas to the detriment of peripheral areas of the world economy. He argued that emigration and core formation had therefore converted 'one part of the globe into a chiefly agricultural field of production for supplying the other part which remains a chiefly industrial field'. He also stressed the importance of surplus pools of labour in rural Ireland and the Scottish Highlands to the development of the industrial and indeed agricultural cores in Britain and North America. Thus he argued that the Highland clearances and the rural exodus from Ireland served identical ends – the creation of viable fields of agricultural production in Scotland and Ireland and the simultaneous transformation of Scotland and Ireland into 'emigrant nurseries'.[11] Certainly by the late-nineteenth century Marx's fatalistic prediction that it was Ireland's national destiny to become 'an English sheepwalk and cattle pasture, her people banished by sheep and ox' had largely come true.[12] It was against this background that Ireland's middling tenantry and the Catholic middle class gradually acquired hegemonic status in the latter half of the nineteenth century.

The Italian Marxist, Antonio Gramsci, used the category 'hegemony' in a socio-historical sense to define 'the moment when objective and subjective forces combine to produce a situation of revolutionary change'.[13] This is the moment when the economic and political structures of the old order collapse and new social forces emerge which have the will, determination and historical insight to take advantage of changing developments in national and international society. This precisely describes socio-political developments in the aftermath of the Famine when a challenging collectivity comprising substantial Catholic tenants and the middle class came of political age and established for themselves a position which enabled them to dominate small farmers and the 'respectable poor' outside the north-east of Ireland.

Writing in an Italian context, Gramsci recognised that a 'hegemony' had distinctive geographical correlates and that it was rooted to particular places.[14] The manner in which the largely peasant Mezzogiorno had been integrated into an Italian state dominated by northern industrialists particularly attracted Gramsci's attention. The latter, he argued, in alliance with southern land-owners and an intelligentsia which operated as intermediaries between peasants and landowners, established hegemonic control over all of Italy in the late-nineteenth century.

Gramsci's approach is particularly suited to an analysis of class configuration, state formation and emigration in post-Famine Ireland for a number of reasons. Firstly, Gramsci recognised the rural poor as important actors in the political arena. In particular he showed how through their links with the petty bourgeoisie, the substantial peasantry and small-farming communities had a debilitating effect on working-class politics and on radical movements for agrarian reform. Secondly, he showed how regionally powerful groups (e.g.

northern industrialists in the case of Italy) exerted control over society at large by forming inter-regional and intranational class alliances. Thirdly, Gramsci explained the anomaly of subordinate social classes being led by a middle-class intelligentsia in terms of the latter's social class origins, particularly their close links with the rural poor and the 'respectable' working class. Thus he showed that the intelligentsia, especially the clergy, functioned as social mediators between dominant and subordinate classes in regionally-differentiated and stratified nation-states. Peasants and small farmers, he argued, frequently also regarded priests, teachers and others set above them in a deeply ambivalent manner. On the one hand they looked up to them as their political 'betters' and 'natural' leaders because so many of them were their own flesh and blood. This was especially the case in the south of Italy and in the west of Ireland where priests, teachers and other petty officials acted as social intermediaries between the rural poor and nation-building classes. Their socially strategic positions also gave this group a disproportionate moral and political influence over Irish rural and working-class communities.

In nineteenth-century Ireland, the indigenous bourgeoisie comprised a wide range of social groups. It included large landholders, middling tenants, 'thirty acre men', the merchant class, industrialists, the 'shopocracy' and the professions. Despite its diverse social origins and the diversity of its political outlook, this group consolidated its hegemonic control by extending its political influence beyond the rich heartlands of rural Ireland and by forming alliances with the petty bourgeoisie along the west and north-west coast.[15] This control was forged on the anvil of land clearances and owed its very existence to Ireland's status as an emigrant nursery and to the systematic removal of the country's surplus workers.

In Ireland, as in colonial societies elsewhere, native propertied elements did not lament the passing of 'traditional' Ireland through emigration and capitalist modernisation. Ever since the Famine they had practised their own crude version of rate-capping and sought to ensure that Poor Law legislation would not pose an obstacle to its programme of rural development under bourgeois/ nationalist hegemony. Like their peers in England and Scotland, they took great care to ensure that Poor Relief would only be distributed to those who had abandoned all claims to land and property. This had the effect of creating a glut of smallholdings on the property market which were rented or bought up by 'improving' tenants and independent farmers. Thus the emptying of the countryside through poverty and emigration greatly extended the geographical range of commercial farming in Ireland and allowed those who stayed behind to add field to field. Similarly, export-led agricultural development later in the century enabled those with viable tenancies to specialise for the market. While this raised the level of agricultural production, it also pushed the 'surplus off-spring' from family farms onto the emigrant trail.

From as early as mid-century the indigenous bourgeoisie had been proclaiming Ireland's right to self-determination and asserting political control over Ireland the emigrant nursery. Catholic middling tenant-farmers, merchants and large farmers in particular, occupied positions of power in the Poor Law institutions established in mid-nineteenth-century Ireland. They were among the chief benefactors of the Famine induced restructuring of Irish property relations and post-Famine induced emigration. Certainly the 'property adjustment' caused by Famine and by Famine induced emigration extended to western small-farming counties by the closing decades of the nineteenth century. As Miller suggests:

> the structural changes in post-Famine developed *in tandem with emigration: they were mutually reinforcing as well as self-perpetuating phenomena.* For example, while it is fair to cite commercialisation of agriculture as emigration's root cause, it is equally true that

> process – involving the engrossment of grassland, the
> switch to impartible inheritance, and the proletarian-
> isation of rural labour – could not have occurred so
> rapidly and thoroughly except as a result of mass
> emigration . . . In short, these processes were circular
> and interdependent.[16] (Emphasis added)

But for the safety-valve of emigration, the movement for agrarian reform in these districts could well have resulted in a fundamental restructuring of Irish property relations in the late-nineteenth and early-twentieth century. As Breathnach suggests, the takeover of this movement by larger farmers from the midlands not only extended the hegemonic status of the latter – it also meant that the objectives of agrarian reform were reduced to the transformation of existing holdings from tenancies to outright proprietorships. As the American recession of the 1870s clearly showed, when the safety-valve of emigration was temporarily stopped, the resultant surplus of young adults in Ireland could fuel rural unrest and give added force to movements for agrarian and social reform.[17] As Breathnach has also shown, the resolution of the land question in favour of substantial tenants had the effect of 'creating a mass of conservative property-owning peasants who have dominated the Irish political scene until recently'.[18] The flood of emigration since then has regularly dampened revolutionary potential in Ireland by removing abroad young adults when they came of political age. By 1901 the socially-strategic 'thirty acre men', the most conservative element in the agrarian reform movement, constituted almost one-third of all Irish farmers.[19] Their hegemonic status was not only reflected in their superior level of organisation – it was reflected also in their claims to have political solutions to the social and economic problems caused by widespread and persistent emigration.

However, on the eve of independence Ireland had become so thoroughly commercialised by 'alien' landlordism and 'native' capitalism that the termination of British political rule in Ireland had minimal structural consequences for the country. It simply involved the transfer of property and power from an 'alien' elite to a native bourgeoisie which, although nominally powerful, had little real control over an economy that was inextricably linked to an economic system which benefited them as a class but was subversive of the general welfare of large numbers of Irish young adults who were forced to emigrate.

Table 1.2: Estimated gross migratory outflows, 1852–1990.

| | Destination | | | Gross Outflow (000s) |
Period	U K	U S	Other Overseas	
1852–61	—	—	—	792
1861–71	—	—	—	697
1871–81	—	—	—	446
1881–91	41	514	62	617
1891–01	17	347	13	377
1901–11	14	240	12	266
1911–22	9	97	10	116
1926–31	n.a.	104	15	n.a.
1931–36	n.a.	2	2	n.a.
1936–41	n.a.	3	2	n.a.
1941–46	173	—	—	173
1946–51	119	17	8	144
1951–61	n.a.	——— 68 ———		n.a.
1961–71	n.a.	——— 49 ———		n.a.
1971–81	155	——— 21 ———		176
1981–90	245	49	64	358

Source: *Economic and Social Implications of Emigration* (National Economic and Social Council, March, 1991), p.58.

Emigration not only consolidated the hegemonic status of the Catholic middle class and the property-owning peasantry, it also contributed to the peripheralisation of rural Ireland while simultaneously fostering the development of core areas in the world economy. With the notable exception of Ulster, internal migration did not contribute in any significant way to the growth of urban cores within Ireland. Instead young adults from rural Ireland were proletarianised into the labour markets of London, Manchester, Liverpool, Boston and New York and many of them may have looked on these cities, rather than Dublin or Belfast, as 'their' capitals. Thus Table 1.3 shows that the Irish made up 10 per cent of the British labour force in the early 1860s. Within Britain they were a very significant ethnic labour force in the expanding cities of the midlands, the north of England and lowland Scotland. As the century progressed this movement of young adults out of the country gradually became an irrevocable move to countries from which there was little prospect of return.[20]

Table 1.3: The Irish in British labour markets, 1787–1871.

Year	Irish-born in Britain (000s)	Irish in Britain (000s)	Irish Labourer (000s)	% British Labour Force
1787	20.0	40.0	22.8	0.58
1821	182.0	365.0	207.7	3.35
1831	290.0	580.0	330.0	4.58
1841	415.7	831.5	473.1	5.63
1851	727.3	1,403.7	779.1	8.03
1861	805.7	1,555.0	950.1	8.80
1871	774.3	1,494.4	913.1	7.61

Source: David Williamson 'The impact of the Irish on British labour markets during the Industrial Revolution', in Swift and Gilley (eds.) The Irish in Britain (London: Barnes and Noble, 1989).

Fitzpatrick has shown that Irish emigration differed in a number of respects from other nineteenth-century migrations. Firstly, although men outnumbered women on pre-Famine emigrant trails, female emigrants outnumbered males throughout the closing decades of the nineteenth and the opening decades of the twentieth century. This was particularly true of young emigrants between fifteen and twenty-four years of age. Secondly, unlike most European migrations which were a mixture of single men and family groups, Irish emigrants were less inclined to emigrate as family groups and were more likely to be unattached women.[21] Indeed, on the eve of World War I, married couples accounted for only one-tenth of Irish emigrants. Thirdly, Irish emigrants tended to be drawn from younger age groups than their European counterparts. Of those who left between 1855 and 1914, between one-third and one-half were between twenty and twenty-four years old, and a significant number of the remainder were teenagers. This meant that emigration after the Famine was deeply embedded in the structure of the Irish family and in the life cycles of young Irish males and females. Fourthly, the great majority of emigrants left Ireland without marketable skills. Fitzpatrick has also unkindly described Irish emigrants in this period as a group who:

> were probably as innumerate and illiterate as the populations from which they sprang. Most of those who left were virtually unencumbered by training, expertise or accomplishment. They emerged from a context of enforced idleness and ignorance full of eagerness to learn how to labour and to serve.[22]

This is an unsympathetic and unkind treatment of Irish emigrants both because it ignores their rich oral traditions and portrays them as an undifferentiated deferential mass.

Although there was a *qualitative* dimension to late-nineteenth and early-twentieth century Irish emigration, the majority of young emigrants started out on the lowest echelons of the international labour force. In areas of Britain and the United States where the Irish were so dominant, there were jobs that became the almost exclusive preserve of the Irish. Road work, the construction industry and domestic service clearly belong to this category. During this period the proportions of labourers and servants seldom fell below 80 per cent of total emigration from Ireland. As Fitzpatrick suggests, this means that the Irish exodus then cannot be depicted as a 'brain drain' or as a drain of 'human capital'.

SEASONAL MIGRANTS AND THE PERSISTENCE OF PEASANT IRELAND

Migrant workers and emigrants from Ireland not only filled gaps in the international demand for labour at crucial stages in the development of global capitalism, they also provided families at home with cash which contributed to the welfare and very survival of small farming and working-class communities into the twentieth century. One Donegal historian put this point well when he argued that 'seasonal earnings helped householders keep their homes'.[23] Handley has estimated that almost 38,000 seasonal migrants were annually leaving Ireland for Britain between 1880 and 1900.[24] An estimated 18,000 seasonal migrants from the west and north-west of the country were still moving between Ireland, Scotland and the north of England on the eve of World War I. Many of those were engaged in 'tattie hoking' and their destinations reflected the need to locate in accessible locations with a high seasonal demand for agricultural labour. This sector of the rural poor may simply have regarded emigration as a geographical extension of 'hiring out' practices. It is therefore not possible to characterise seasonal migration to Scotland and England in the late-nineteenth and early-twentieth century as a search for a higher standard of living or as the product of the rising expectations on the part of Irish youth. O'Gráda rightly asserts that it is far more realistic to see it as a crucial part of the struggle for subsistence. 'Scottish money' – the remittances which young Irish emigrants sent home from Scotland – often accounted for one-quarter of the cash income of poor families in parts of the west and north-west of Ireland up to World War I.[25] Fitzpatrick estimates that Mayo's 10,000 or so migratory workers sent home more than £100,000 annually between 1876 and 1880.[26] However, although seasonal migration in Ireland, as indeed in Spain, Portugal, Turkey and Greece, helped sustain small farming communities well into the twentieth century, the negative effects of emigration were more obvious than its localised positive effects.[27] As one commentator asserted on the eve of World War I, emigration contributed to the 'perpetual survival of the unfittest' and the 'steady debasement of the human currency' in Ireland.[28]

2. OFFICIAL ATTITUDES TO IRISH EMIGRATION IN THE NINETEENTH CENTURY

THE MALTHUSIAN DEFENSE OF DISAPPEARING IRELAND

The transition around the 1870s from theories of emigration to theories of colonisation was a very important turning point, not only in British, but also in Irish attitudes to emigration. It coincided with the emergence of disciplined nationalist movements in Ireland and the revival of interest in Britain's imperial role. It also encouraged a sanitised view of the New World as the best place for the *Celtic* race, especially for those among them who could never hope to secure a living within Ireland.

Political attitudes to Irish emigration have long been refracted through ethnic and social class lenses. They have also shaped and been shaped by prevailing political orthodoxies, particularly by nationalist attitudes to Ireland's place in the international community.[29] Malthusianists on both sides of the Irish Sea regarded Ireland's rural exodus as a precondition for capitalist modernisation. By the 1880s Irish emigration was widely perceived as a 'mathematical demonstration' which showed that the best which could be done for the rural poor 'was to emigrate them altogether'.[30] From as early as the mid-nineteenth century, Malthusianists were also advocating state support for Irish emigration and suggesting that those leaving Ireland were faring well outside it. They also countered radical interpretations of emigration as a cruel response to 'rancherism' by arguing that emigration was caused by Ireland's proximity to Britain and by revolutions in transportation which drew Ireland closer to Britain and the United States, where, political conservatives argued, the 'troublesome Irish' belonged.[31]

Malthusian defenders of emigration as a solution to over-population in 'Congested Ireland' also advocated emigration as a solution to the problems of rural underdevelopment. After considering the options available for the alleviation of poverty along the Atlantic fringe of Ireland, one state official argued:

> *What seems to be needed for the relief of these districts is the establishment on a permanent basis of an emigration department*, which, with a competent staff, and the co-operation of a voluntary committee, combined with systematic and careful oversight at ports of departure and arrival, shall from year to year, and not spasmod-ically, deal with all applications for assisted emigration, and advise or make grants in each case as may seem for the best.[32]

These sentiments were echoed throughout rural Ireland. What made them all the more remarkable was the fact that they referred to subjects of the Crown in Ireland in terms reminiscent of the racism, paternalism and ethnocentrism normally reserved for subordinate communities in colonial Africa and India. In the event, many of the rural poor vanished from the country, running off to England, Scotland, and North America 'with hardly enough English to write their names'.[33]

It is important to note that Malthusian justifications for emigration transcended ethnic divisions in nineteenth-century Ireland. Thus the middling tenantry and Catholic priests in impoverished regions throughout Ireland often looked on emigration as an acceptable solution to the poverty of landless families and the cottier classes. Although they could not couch their support for emigration quite so radically or paternalistically as their colonial overlords, they nevertheless realised that the scattering of Mother Ireland's *poorest* sons and daughters was in everyone's interests. This was particularly true of Catholic priests in the 'congested' west coast where emigration was often perceived as the *only* solution to rural destitution. Irish social and political leaders here frequently hinted that any long-term curtailment of emigration was impossible because it ran counter to the 'natural' forces of the market and the natural principles of political economy.

NATIONALIST CRITIQUE AND HISTORICIST REACTIONS

In order to make political capital from the fact that entire tracts of Ireland were being cleared to make room for 'English graziers and their bullocks', nationalists were compelled to ignore the structuring role of emigration in making room for the family farms of the indigenous tenantry.[34] Instead they *Anglicised* the causes of Irish emigration and *nationalised* its solutions. They also systematically refuted each assimilationist premise underlying the progressive Anglicisation of post-Famine Ireland and attributed emigration solely to 'landlordism', 'rancherism' and 'English misrule' in Ireland. Rudimentary though it was, this historicist reaction to colonial rule in Ireland revolutionised social attitudes towards Irish emigration. It also problematised a wide range of other social and economic issues that were supposed to have been resolved through the operation of the *laissez-faire* principles of English political economy in colonial Ireland.[35] Irish nationalists subverted this discourse by arguing that Anglo-Irish rancherism was the major cause of Irish emigration and that the English political economy provided *ideological* justification for the modernisation of agriculture which caused such widespread emigration. They also attacked as erroneous the assumption that rancherism was necessarily more productive than *petit culture*.[36] They insisted that large scale agriculture based on the great estates should give way to *petit culture*, initially centred on the tenant-holding and subsequently on the family-owned farm. They also suggested that Britain was engaged in a subtle exercise in social engineering in Ireland and that the British government sought to remove the Irish abroad when they were most needed to construct an Irish nation at home.[37]

According to this 'narrow nationalist' viewpoint, landlordism alone was responsible for emigration and emigrants were victims of alien oppression by 'tyrants' who drove the Irish from their 'happy home'. Indeed in nation-building circles the whole question of Ireland's declining population and involuntary emigration was charged with emotion and linked to the controversy of the 'vanishing Irish' and 'Irish extermination'. However the view of emigration taken from the pulpit often differed from that taken from the farm gate. While church leaders worried that emigration was becoming a 'kind of self-defacement' and stressed the destructive effects of emigration on local business and community life, small tenant farmers and improving landlords regarded it as a safety-valve which eased pressure on the land and on the country's unevenly distributed resources. At best they hoped that emigration would place Irish young adults on a better footing outside than they could ever hope to attain inside the country. As we have already seen, some priests (particularly in 'congested districts') took the view that some level of emigration was unavoidable in the case of young adults from impoverished large families, and argued that it was an acceptable solution to the certainty of misery and poverty experienced by such families within Ireland. This meant that many priests viewed emigration through the prism of social class which tempered their nationalism and suggested that the 'new Ireland' was to be built by the 'hale and hearty sons' of the rural bourgeoisie, not by the sons and daughters of the rural and urban poor. In so doing they suggested that the latter should accept emigration as a *natural alternative* to lack of work at home. Miller has well described the contradictory attitudes to emigration in nation-building Ireland as follows:

> [Blame] for emigration reflected nationalists' and clerics' tortuous efforts *to reconcile traditional social ideals and their own hegemonic imperatives with a social reality which violated those ideals and yet paradoxically both sustained and threatened that hegemony.* On the one hand, many Catholic spokesmen realized that only massive lower class emigration had created the relatively commercialized, urbanized, and bourgeois-dominated 'New Ireland', which had been the precondition for the success of disciplined nationalist movements and the church's devotional revolution . . . In addition, Catholic spokesmen also understood that emigration brought specific material benefits to some key elements in Irish society as well as, they hoped, to the emigrants themselves.[38] (Emphasis added)

Church leaders and nationalists also stressed the destructive effects of emigration on the social and cultural fabric of rural Ireland. In particular they contrasted the pre-Famine emigration of 'pale and panic-stricken people' with the exodus of 'stalwart, muscular, dauntless young braves' leaving Ireland in the late-nineteenth and early-twentieth century. These, they asserted, were 'royally endowed with every attitude that goes to make up a peerless and magnificent manhood' and their going was depriving nation-building Ireland of its very 'bone and sinew'.[39] They argued that emigration in the late-nineteenth century did not simply involve farm labourers or artisans. It also took away farmers' sons 'who preferred the bustle of life in America to the monotony of country life at home'.[40] Unlike the 'sad, weeping and melancholy emigrants' of the 'Hungry Forties', these new emigrants 'did not carry with them one single reminder of their nationality'. Instead they were 'casting off all allegiance to the land' and when they left 'one heard no longer the shout of an everlasting farewell but a ringing cheer'. It was feared that these emigrants were becoming a source of envy to those left behind on the land, many of whom looked at their 'fortunate friends escaping' and hoped that 'when the letter and passage money arrive, they too will be able to leave this land of bondage and follow their friends to the promised land in the wake of the setting sun'.[41] Nationalists were also alarmed by the fact that emigration had become so far advanced that it was becoming a voluntary activity which attracted 'the athletic male population'. Like critics of middle-class emigration today, they were equally concerned about the *quality* and the *volume* of Irish emigration, with some leaders even arguing that the genetic pool of the Irish race would literally run dry through emigration. Church leaders also suggested that emigration was depriving Catholic Ireland of its 'breeding stock' because it was attracting country girls who 'sacrificed their dowries and a certain prospect of marriage for the pleasure of serving in a business house in New York or even going into a situation as housemaids in American families'.[42] Not surprisingly, a whole genre of literature emerged in late-nineteenth and early-twentieth century Ireland which portrayed emigration as the product of 'alien' rule and suggested that some form of self-government would solve Ireland's social and economic problems.

3. IRISH EMIGRATION FROM 1921 TO THE 1980S

RURAL FUNDAMENTALISM AND THE PERSISTENCE OF EMIGRATION

Independence confirmed the hegemonic status of the rural bourgeoisie and De Valera's Ireland was a society characterised by a high degree of rural fundamentalism which prioritised rural and small-town values over urban values. These in turn informed social and economic policy in Ireland right up to the 1960s. Thus Commins has argued that Irish rural fundamentalism involved a positive view of farming as an occupation and a positive view of the family farm as the basic unit of agricultural production. This also meant that agriculture was to be the basis of national prosperity in Ireland and that government policy would prioritise the interests of farmers over those of industrialists, the working class and fishermen, *the* most neglected sector of Irish society. Commins has also suggested that rural fundamentalism in Ireland found some of its basis in Catholic ethical and social thought in that it advocated the diffusion of property and emphasised 'the intrinsic value of agricultural work, together with the desirability of owner-occupied farms'.[43] He showed that the most cogent expression of fundamentalist values was contained in the Minority Report to the Commission on Emigration drawn up in the early 1950s by Bishop Lucey of Cork. Lucey called for the growth of Dublin to be halted, for ownership of land to be widely diffused, for the rural home to be kept as the optimum place for raising a family, and for farm holdings to be kept between fifteen and twenty acres.[44]

However in Ireland, as in peripheral states elsewhere in the world economy, the holders of political power had little *real* control over an economy still exposed to the structuring forces of international capitalism. In the event Ireland remained highly-dependent upon Britain both as a market for her exports and as a host to her 'surplus' sons and daughters. Indeed the relationships between the British and Irish economies remained so close after the 'economic war' of the Thirties that population movements from Ireland to England were part of a broader general process of rural-urban drift.[45]

Table 3.1: Estimated Irish emigration, 1926–1966.

Years	Annual Average
1926–1936	16,000
1936–1946	18,000
1946–1951	24,000
1951–1956	39,000
1956–1961	42,000
1961–1966	16,000

Source: John Kennedy, The Irish in Britain (Routledge and Kegan Paul, 1973).

Hazelkorn has emphasised the political dimension of this drift from the land in Ireland to urban centres in Britain by arguing that Irish young adults voted with their feet in their thousands to abandon De Valera's narrow nationalist dream of an Irish people 'satisfied with a frugal comfort and devoted to the things of the spirit'.[46]

World War II also emphasised the strong dependence of Britain on Ireland for surplus labour. Thus Lennon, McAdam and O'Brien have argued:

> During the war Britain *needed to supplement its labour force and it automatically turned to its traditional source, Ireland. This dramatically underlined the extent to which the economic relationship between the two countries remained unchanged by political independence.* The Irish state was officially neutral – in practice it was 'neutral on England's side'. Thousands of Irish men and women, from north and south of the border, joined the British Army. Many more left for Britain, directly recruited by the British authorities to fill the gaps in the labour

force. Recruitment posters appeared in the labour exchanges in Ireland urging women to join the forces, apply for jobs and come and help the war effort. Given its own economic problems, the Fianna Fáil government turned a blind eye, and went along with the option of exporting its surplus labour. Many women found that the war presented them with opportunities they would have been denied in more normal times. By the end of the war, the numbers of Irish women in Britain in nursing, factory work and clerical work were rising, and the numbers in domestic work were falling. (Emphasis added)[47]

Emigration on this scale was clearly not caused by Ireland's geographical proximity to Britain. As Carol Coulter has suggested, Ireland's geographical location and level of economic development did not explain Ireland's political institutions or its class structure. These were defined instead by:

> our historically defined place in international relations and the political institutions we have inherited from the past, themselves the accumulation of battles fought between different social forces.[48]

Although its location relative to Britain did not inevitably cause the Irish Free State to function as an emigrant nursery for the British economy, it nevertheless compounded the process of peripheralisation in Ireland by relieving the Irish state of the responsibility for solving unemployment and lack of opportunity at home. This in turn was exacerbated by differentials in the level of development in Ireland, particularly the low level of urban development, and by levels of development in Britain and the United States. It was aggravated also by the fact that reductions in the relative costs of emigrating from Ireland from the late-nineteenth century onwards have always made it easy for Ireland's surplus workers to leave Ireland for Britain and North America.

Table 3.2: Number of persons who received travel permits, identity cards and passports between 1940 and 1951 in order to take up employment, classified by broad occupation.

Occupation	(000s)	%
Males		
Unskilled	113.3	53.1
Agricultural	43.2	20.3
Industrial	27.6	12.9
Other	29.3	13.7
Total	**213.4**	**100.0**
Females		
Domestic services	85.5	57.2
Nursing	20.8	13.9
Agricultural	3.8	2.5
Clerical	3.6	2.4
Other	35.9	24.0
Total	**149.6**	**100.0**

Source: Commission on Emigration (1954).

Despite nationalist promises to the contrary, independence did not make Ireland a country fit for young men, let alone for young women. Instead, as Breathnach has argued, emigration continued to characterise relations between Ireland and the English-speaking world well into the 1950s.[49] By then also the potential for developing an indigenous industrial base was already severely weakened, not least by the exodus of skilled and unskilled workers. Emphasising the positive functions of large-scale emigration in post-independence Ireland, Raymond Crotty has claimed that:

> Emigration has given to Ireland . . . conditions approximating to 'full employment', with no large pool of unemployed labour to form a source of competing

non-unionised labour, working either as self-employed persons or for non-union firms. These virtually 'full employment' conditions, brought about by mass emigration, have been fundamentally different from normal conditions of massive growing labour surpluses in the former capitalist colonies.[50]

He also suggests that union aggression since the '60s *contributed* to Irish emigration by forcing wages above levels acceptable to employers. It could equally be argued that employers benefited from the labour surpluses in 'emigrant blackspots' where young adults preferred low wages and poor promotional opportunities at home to the unwelcome option of emigration. Certainly the long-term unemployed in Ireland since World War II have not only comprised those made redundant by seasonal, technical or trade factors – they have also included those unwilling, or unable, to emigrate. Much more research is needed to establish the truth of Crotty's assertion that the 'double selection' of people unable to find work in Ireland, and those unwilling to leave it, has meant that 'the hard core of long-term Irish unemployed was of exceptionally poor quality and offered little if any threat to the privileged position of employed trade unionists'.[51]

IRELAND – THE EMIGRANT NURSERY AND THE POST-WAR ECONOMY

It is certainly possible to argue that cheap labour from Ireland has contributed to the regeneration of capitalism and core formation in Britain and the United States since World War II. Ready access to labour pools in Ireland has also regularly reduced Britain's overdependence on migrant labour from ex-colonies in the Third World. This has helped Britain contain her race-relations problem by curtailing the number of migrant workers from Africa, the Caribbean and Asia. This has also meant that post-war Britain was not as dependent upon migrant labour from ex-colonies in the Third World as Germany and France clearly have been. Unlike both these countries, Britain never had to develop a *Gastarbeiter* or 'guest-worker' system of labour recruitment in order to resolve its labour deficit problems; it could simply rely upon Irish immigrants and migrant workers.

After World War II the social geography and occupational structure of Irish immigrants in Britain differed in important respects from that of their predecessors. As access to the American labour market grew increasingly restrictive, the Irish now moved to the midlands and south-east of England where a new 'emigrant aristocracy' developed as a result of war-induced shortages of skilled and professional labour. The Irish also benefited from the post-war expansion of the welfare state in Britain and now moved into new sectors of white-collar employment like nursing, teaching and clerical work. By the '60s, Irish graduates with qualifications in engineering, medicine and law were probably regarding Britain and Ireland as an integrated labour market.

Economic developments within Ireland were also contributing to the curtailment of Irish emigration. However, while export-led industrialisation temporarily reversed emigration in the '60s and '70s in some parts of Ireland at least, it did not alter the *peripheral status* of the Irish state. As Breathnach rightly points out, the '60s simply saw a shifting in the axis of dependency from Britain to the United States and mainland Europe, as Ireland had clearly become highly dependent upon foreign-owned firms. By the mid-'70s these employed over a third of the entire workforce in manufacturing industry in the country.[52] Ireland then was also heavily dependent on high-tech and capital intensive industries which often left the country as soon as tax-free holidays ended.[53]

Taking electronics as an example, Murray and Wickham have shown that the '70s witnessed a dual dependent industrialisation and technologisation of Irish economic development. The expansion of new industrial sectors, particularly electronics, pharmaceuticals, computers and electrical engineering was not a natural development caused by the decomposition of the labour process within more traditional labour intensive industries. Neither was it simply the product of increased competition for production sites between Ireland, Scotland, Wales and the north of England. These sectors were promoted as an expression of 'institutionalised ideology'. They were developed in the interests of 'nativising' foreign technology by 'an ostentatious display of strategic planning by state agencies responsible for industrial development and manpower policy'.[54] Crowley suggests that Ireland's peripheral location in the New International Division of Labour has been created and fostered by these multinational corporations, and by state agencies since the '70s. She also shows that multinational corporations usually located here only those phases of the production process which required smaller quantities and low quality of labour, and that the expanding sectors of manufacturing industry in Ireland were 'primary arenas for female proletarianisation'.[55] Dependent industrialisation also had other results. It gave Ireland a more diversified economy and created a significant degree of occupational segregation and regional differentiation in the country. As Wickham has argued, it also mixed mastery of technology with technical awe and national pride, to produce a false sense of autonomy which suggested that these industries allowed the nation to recover economic sovereignty.[56]

While this altered the ownership and composition of industry in Ireland and gave the country the image of a technologically-advanced society, new capital intensive industries did not absorb the country's sizeable labour surpluses or reduce dependence on overseas labour markets for disposing of those who were unemployed or unable to achieve social mobility at home.[57] Neither did they close the substantial gap separating Ireland from the core areas of the world economy. Instead Ireland, like Greece, Scotland, Portugal,

Spain and Italy, retained the dual status of an 'emigrant nursery' and peripheral state. Young adults left these countries not just because they were possessed of a 'spirit of adventure', they left because the supply of labour exceeded demand and because opportunities for economic and social advancement were restricted by the peripheral status and class structure of these comparatively underdeveloped states.

Thus in the '80s 'new wave' emigration from Ireland coincided with a downturn in the industrial economy which marked a turning point in Irish industrial development. Manufacturing employment alone dropped from 243,000 in 1980 to 201,000 by 1986, thus constituting the longest sustained decline in manufacturing industry in Ireland since the foundation of the State.[58] This, rather than the 'enterprise culture' of Irish young adults, is the proper starting point for an analysis of the structural roots of 'new wave' Irish emigration.

4. THE SANITISATION AND 'DE-NATIONALISATION' OF IRISH EMIGRATION

Although the social composition, destinations and political and economic functions of Irish emigration have not altered all that much in recent decades, Irish attitudes to emigration have certainly altered significantly since the late-nineteenth century. Since at least the 1960s, Irish emigration has also been 'de-nationalised' and naturalised by revisionists who have substituted nationalist condemnations of emigration as an indictment of 'English misrule' in colonial Ireland for cost-benefit analyses of its impact on Irish society and its contribution to the Irish 'diaspora' overseas.

Economists and historians in particular have treated Irish emigration as a socially progressive response to the modernisation of an island economy on the periphery of Europe.[59] Indeed, since the '60s, the 'blame Britain' ethos of nationalist condemnations of emigration has given way to behavioural and geographical explanations of its causes and consequences. There is an increasing tendency today to treat emigration as a cultural tradition and a voluntary activity which attracts upwardly mobile individuals who are assumed to be leaving Ireland to climb social ladders abroad. The voluntarisation and sanitisation of Irish emigration is also evident in historical accounts. In his monumental *Emigrants and Exiles* Kirby Miller therefore suggests:

> Despite the prevalence and persistence of the exile image, comparatively few emigrants were compelled by force or famine to leave Ireland, particularly between 1856 and 1921, when most departures occurred. Rather *the Irish emigrated voluntarily in order to better themselves*; and at least in theory they could have remained in Ireland, as many of their spokesmen advocated . . . In short, there seems no rational reason inherent in either the actual circumstances of most emigrant's departures or the material conditions of Irish-American life which automatically translated into a homesickness perhaps common to all emigrants into a morbid perception of themselves as involuntary emigrants, passive victims of English oppression. (Emphasis added)[60]

This author traced the 'homesickness' of Irish emigrants to a peculiarly Irish attachment to their own homeland and kith and kin. He also suggests that emigration-as-exile is rooted in a traditional worldview which predisposed Irish emigrants to 'perceive or at least justify themselves not as voluntary, ambitious emigrants but as involuntary, irresponsible "exiles", compelled to leave home by forces beyond individual control, particularly by British and landlord oppression'.[61] In so arguing, Miller not only charges emigrants with possession of false consciousness, he also allows the historian of emigration, rather than emigrants themselves, to determine whether or not there were many among the millions who left Ireland between 1856 and 1921 who genuinely considered themselves exiles from Ireland. Like others in what is essentially a historical revisionist tradition, Miller views Irish emigrants as rational actors who carefully consider all available openings before making migratory decisions and treats as free choices decisions which were in fact structured by social and economic forces operating within Ireland and at the level of the world economy.

David Lloyd on the other hand has argued that it is possible to criticise nationalist categorisations of the overseas Irish as a 'diaspora' without having to voluntarise or sanitise Irish emigration to the extent that Miller does. However like Miller, Lloyd also hesitates to apply the term 'diaspora' to the Irish in America because they are such an integrated element of contemporary white American society. He adds:

> Return is no longer a powerful emotional idea for Irish Americans, except in the mostly sentimental and fetishising desire to establish their genealogy in the old country. That desire has been augmented recently by the successes of liberal 'multiculturalism', which has left many white Americans, whose roots are now twisted and entangled in the soil of several European lands, seeking the cultural distinctiveness that they have learned to be the privilege of ethnic minorities.[62]

Lloyd also suggests that the invocation of an 'Irish diaspora' has had the effect of 'naturalising the continuing outflow of skilled and unskilled labour from Ireland, as if there were some given population level for the island that we have already exceeded'.[63]

In stressing the inevitability of emigration, historical revisionists and modernisation theorists have also de-politicised the causes of Irish emigration. Thus, unlike their Scottish, Welsh, and English counterparts, Irish historians have been poor defenders of the 'moral economy' of rural and working-class communities which have regularly been devastated by emigration. Indeed contemporary attitudes to Irish emigration reflect a serious devaluation of nationalism as a philosophy informing social and economic policy in Ireland. Today nationalism has been so seriously 'narrowed' that it has been almost exclusively associated with Republicanism and political violence in Northern Ireland. Mary Holland recently suggested that nationalism in Ireland today is almost 'an embarrassment' and is seen to have been contaminated by its association with political violence in Northern Ireland.[64] In the Republic of Ireland at least, nationalism has been transformed into what Nell McCafferty aptly calls 'a love that dare not speak its name', and is increasingly seen as something which must be kept 'decently hidden'. This reluctance to examine the contemporary significance of nationalism, together with a concern with our image as a modern state, has meant that we are more concerned about attracting high-tech industry and tourists to Ireland than thinking about ways of blocking the haemorrhage of young adults from the country.

THE GLOBALISATION OF IRISH SOCIETY

The devaluation of nationalism as a political ideology informing social and economic and not just constitutional policy is not peculiar to Ireland. It is a European-wide phenomenon which in Ireland's case is literally influencing the way we see ourselves in the world. It has also contributed to the 'de-territorialisation' of politics across western Europe. Like other small ethno-nations, particularly those on the peripheries of Europe, we have experienced severe curtailments of our national sovereignty as a concomitant of our deeper integration into the European Union and the global economy. As elsewhere in Europe, and particularly in Scotland, Wales, Italy and Greece, this has had the effect of weakening local authority and transforming nation-states into glorified local authorities within a larger Europe. Peripheral regions have also been experiencing a transformation of their political cultures with the increase in the number of 'non-territorial' political and social actors operating within their boundaries. This has radically altered the sovereignty and even the territorial status of small nations as *containers* of social, economic and cultural life.

Fundamental changes in the territorial organisation of these societies have been interpreted as evidence of 'time-space compression' because they involve a shift from a 'space of places' to a 'space of flows'.[65] However this view not only 'devalues' places by de-territorialising social phenomena and suggesting that places no longer matter and that home is literally anywhere – it also suggests that we are living in such a period of intense upheaval that we are witnessing the deconstruction of national allegiances, the break-up of local identities and the violent compression of space into time. Revolutions in telecommunications, the 'coca-colaisation' of youth culture, the heightened mobility and flexibility of multinational capital and the dismantling of borders that hitherto *contained* social practices within clearly identifiable territories are all taken as evidence of this process. One globalisation theorist recently argued that changes affecting the borders between territorial communities today have been so far-reaching that they have blurred traditional divisions between 'domestic affairs' and 'foreign affairs'.[66] Others have argued that this has influenced traditional divisions between 'domestic' and 'foreign policy' and radically altered distinctions between 'native' and 'foreigner', and between 'homeland' and 'foreign parts'. Thus, it is argued, with the growing spatial mobility of people across regional, national and supranational borders, it is increasingly difficult to determine who *belongs* in specific places, even though, according to the ultra right at least, it is becoming increasingly obvious who the 'other' is and who does *not belong* in Europe, and in Ireland. The French sociologist Etienne Balibar, in tracing the structural roots of racism in Europe to changing relations between the old colonial powers and the Third World since World War II, has argued:

> the 'two humanities' which have been culturally and socially separated by capitalist development – opposites figuring in racist ideology as 'sub men' and 'supermen', 'underdeveloped' and 'overdeveloped' – do not remain external to each other, kept apart by long distances and related only 'at the margins'. On the contrary, they interpenetrate more and more within the same space of communications, representations and life.[67]

All of these developments have also impacted upon Irish society and influenced the way we see ourselves in relation to others. As we have already seen, the sons and daughters of small-farming and working-class families have always been far more prone to emigrate than those from the middle class. Unlike most other European societies however, the abandonment of Keynesian goals of full employment in Ireland has *not* given rise to grassroots nationalism. Neither has it given renewed significance to traditional myths of 'blood and soil' or sought to exclude the 'foreigner' by preserving 'native' society and traditional culture.

As I have argued here, there is nothing particularly *modern* about the openness of Irish society or about the encounter between the colonised and the coloniser in the case of Ireland. However that openness was deepened throughout the latter half of the nineteenth century and has acquired new significance since the mid-1980s. The accelerated de-territorialisation of Irish society in recent years has caused writers like Fintan O'Toole to suggest that we are witnessing the disappearance of traditional Ireland 'under the pressures of economics, of geography, of the collapse of the religious monolith which was inseparable from our self-definition'.[68] The problem with this view is that it inadvertently contributes to the naturalisation and sanitisation of 'new wave' emigration by arguing that Ireland has now become a radically open society which *naturally* 'lets in the great tide of international blandness and it lets out much of the life blood of the country'.[69] In the event, O'Toole argues, we are left with a peculiarly exposed society, one where Leopold Bloom's gravely diluted definition of a nation as the 'same people' living in 'different places' applies. This de-territorialised view of the nation, which sees contemporary Ireland scattered across the globe, is remarkably close to that of mainstream globalisation theory which argues that:

> home is no longer just one place. It is locations. Home is that place which enables and promotes varied and everchanging perspectives, a place where one discovers new ways of seeing reality, frontiers of difference. One confronts and accepts dispersal and fragmentation as part of the construction of a new world order that reveals more fully where we are, who we can become.[70]

However the problem with these 'devaluations' of home and nation is not just that they naturalise emigration by treating it simply as a dispersal of young adults across a culturally homogeneous world plane. They tell us little about the social composition of emigration and tell us even less about the factors which determine who should, or who should not, stay at home. In particular they ignore the social class and ethnic implications of emigration and ignore the fact that Irish emigration has regularly impacted far more strongly on working-class and small-farming families than on middle-class families, although these have also been affected by emigration.

The history of emigration, class configuration and state formation in Ireland attests to the radical openness of Irish society since at least the nineteenth century. The Anglicisation and commercialisation of Ireland through the extension of the spatial framework of interdependence linking Ireland to Britain has an even longer history. Society, politics, culture and landscape here have been responding to the globalising force of a dynamic British capitalism from at least the sixteenth century onwards. However the globalisation, Americanisation and Europeanisation of Irish society has accelerated tremendously since the 1960s, not least as a result of the substitution of nationalism as a politics of 'mutual exclusiveness' for a uniformity of social standards and a common culture. Again Fintan O'Toole has argued that Irish society has become all the more permeable in recent years because so many young Irish people suffer from a peculiar sense of internal exile which makes them feel increasingly less at home in Ireland.[71]

As I have stressed here, however, this is by no means a new development. Like their nineteenth-century predecessors, many young adults in Ireland today probably regard this country as 'unreal' and 'unrecognisable'. Unlike many of their peers in unemployment blackspots in Britain, France, Spain and Belgium for example, they regard emigration as a natural response to economic recession in Ireland. This has prompted O'Toole to suggest that:

> we should stop using the word 'conservative' about ourselves. We are not a conservative people, we are a fatalistic one [because] Irish young people are prepared to put up with any amount of personal discontinuity rather than contemplate a radically altered future in their own country.[72]

For O'Toole, emigration is the great guarantor of continuity in Irish political life today. We continue to regard emigration as 'the badge of our identity' because familiar cultural markers like the Irish language and Irish Catholicism, and dreams of economic self-sufficiency, political independence, and Irish unification have rapidly melted since our entry into Europe.[73]

In Ireland's case, changes in the political and territorial organisation of society since our entry into the European Community have been so far-reaching that they constitute a radical discontinuity with the traditional view of Ireland as a self-governing and identifiable territorial community. John Waters recently put this very well when he argued that:

> One way of describing what has been happening in Ireland in the past 20 years or so would be to say that the country has been going out of fashion. I do not mean that it has become unfashionable to be Irish, but that the realities of what it is like to live in Ireland and the aspects of Irish life which might ensure the health and stability of future life here have all been rendered unfashionable within the public imagination of the State.[74]

In our anxiety to become 'modern' or 'European', he argues, we have denied ourselves the ability to survive at all. Quoting Milan Kundera, Waters concludes that we have 'become the allies of our own gravediggers', a particularly apt perception of the effects of emigration on Irish society and our attitudes to it.

The devaluation of national and indeed local authority has also generated a new political culture of dependency in peripheral regions in the European Community. As Kevin Whelan has convincingly argued:

> This creates a dependency syndrome, stifling local initiatives and responses, encouraging a grants mentality and a sense of persuasive civic apathy. At the centre, it tends to clog the administrative system with a plethora of detail more efficiently handled at the local level. It also creates a mandarin class, shielded from democratic responsibility or accountability and wrapped in what Tom Barrington has called 'a cocoon of complacent centralisation.' . . . Such a system puts immense pressure on the politician to act predominantly as a

> broker, a handler and a fixer, continuously interposed,
> like a tangler at a fair, between the state and its
> citizens.[75]

He also adds:

> The tendency has been to remove decision-making from
> the hands of elected officials and place it increasingly
> in the hands of appointed ones, making national
> bureaucracy the only effective link between the EC
> and local communities. The lack of effective local
> administration has created a vacuum at the regional
> level, which in turn has inhibited integrated approaches
> to economic development and encouraged sectorally-
> based decision making at the centre.[76]

The deterioration of *national* politics and the new culture of
dependency have not only affected attitudes towards 'new wave'
Irish emigration – they have also affected patterns of emigration as
more and more Irish young adults think in terms of Europe and
mobility when considering solutions to the lack of work and
opportunities at home. Indeed this perception that Europe is an
untilled field of opportunity is deeply embedded in contemporary
Irish youth enterprise culture. A recent handbook for Irish
emigrants stated:

> Europe is now wide open, the economic borders are
> down, labour and money are allowed to move freely and
> emigration has become simply migration. The reality is
> somewhat different. Single market or no single market,
> it's clear that the majority of European states are far
> from ready – and won't be for a long time. In fact, the
> politicians are already admitting in private that it will
> take several years after 1993 to see a borderless Europe.
> Even so, all over the continent, workers, especially
> young people, are swotting up on foreign languages,
> preparing to take a leap in the dark.[77]

DISLOCATING IRISH YOUNG ADULTS

The devaluation of nationalism together with the dislocations caused by the loss of a national sense of place, and a sense of nationalist identity in the Irish Republic, are particularly obvious in changing attitudes to 'new wave' Irish emigration. This in turn has caused Irish political leaders to embrace *modernisation through Europeanisation* as the legitimate object of Irish politics. For many of these, the road to Irish prosperity today runs through Brussels, not Dublin. Since at least the 1960s these same political leaders have been explaining away Irish emigration in terms of Ireland's geographical peripherality within the European Community.

Joe Lee has suggested that simple geographical explanations of, and indeed solutions for, Irish social and economic problems have acquired added force in recent years. Thus he suggests:

> Our current favourite grievance seems to concern our peripheral location. The semantic coinage of 'peripheral' has appreciated considerably since the possibility of procuring compensation for it from Brussels has now come to our attention. Now that our grievances against history are r...ding, we need to nurture a grievance against geography.[78]

Indeed nothing better indicates the 'narrowing' of nationalism to an almost exclusive focus on constitutional issues than the growing acceptance of emigration by Irish political leaders as entirely natural and traditional.[79] In a now famous interview given during an upswing in 'new wave' emigration, Brian Lenihan stated: 'we should not be defeatist or pessimistic about [emigration]. We should be proud about it. After all, we can't all live on a small island'.[80] Lenihan went on to suggest that:

> We regard emigrants as part of our global generation. We should be proud of them. The more they hone their skills and talents in another environment, the more

40

they develop a work ethic in a country like Germany
or the US, the better it can be applied in Ireland when
they return.[81]

The sanitisation and gentrification of 'new wave emigration' since the
'80s is particularly evident in Brian Lenihan's categorisation of the
Irish abroad as our new 'global generation'. Thus he argued:

> I don't look on the type of emigration we have today as
> being in the same category as the terrible emigration in
> the last century. What we have now is a very literate
> emigrant who thinks nothing of going to the United
> States and going back to Ireland and maybe on to
> Germany and back to Ireland again. The world is now
> one world and they can always return to Ireland with
> the skills they have developed.[82]

Another leading Irish education planner with the World Bank recently
argued that:

> If we are true EEC members and we believe in
> European integration, we should see the increasing
> manpower shortage in Europe as a fortuitous oppor-
> tunity for our young people facing unemployment to
> think of 'mobility' and 'migration' as natural solutions.[83]

The illusion that emigration now is simply migration across an
'unboundaried' Europe is particularly obvious in these statements
which certainly contribute to the naturalisation of emigration and
the devaluation of Irish nationalism. They have also caused 'new
wave' emigration to be interpreted as a voluntary movement of
highly-qualified young adults out of this country and into what
Charles Haughey characterised as 'the benign taxfields' of Europe
and the United States. Criticising this view of emigration as a
domestic response to the opening of opportunities abroad, Gearóid
Ó Tuathaigh has insisted that:

This rhetoric of opportunity needs to be interrogated very carefully in the light of the historical experience of Irish emigration. The precise skill and qualifications for which the wider Community market may offer opportunities to Irish workers need to be examined carefully. The underlying logic of the single market (in terms of core – periphery contrasts for example) the ameliorative role of credit transfers through the European Social Fund and regional and structural funds, the precise meaning of the commitment to 'regional development' within the European Community; these and other aspects of the post-1992 vision must be carefully examined in terms of the implications for employment and living standards for workers, in particular for Irish workers who wish to live and work in Ireland. Moreover, the cultural distance which must be travelled for various social categories of Irish workers who may wish to work in other European Community countries has neither been mapped nor measured up to the present time (clearly there is more involved here than language acquisition, however important that may be).[84]

'NEW WAVE' EMIGRATION AND IRISH YOUTH ENTERPRISE CULTURE

We have already seen that, despite its volume and social class composition, conventional wisdom today tends to individualise emigration by treating emigrants as enterprising individuals rather than social groups victimised as a result of structural changes in Irish society, including structural changes in the relationship between Ireland and overseas labour markets. There is also a tendency today to treat young emigrants as individuals set apart from their predecessors by their superior skills, and from their peers by their spirit of adventure.

Government officials in particular have promoted this image of 'new wave' emigration as a voluntary activity involving young adults who have qualified themselves out of the Irish labour market by qualifying themselves into the labour markets of Europe and the United States. They have also suggested that emigration is so deeply embedded in the Irish psyche that it is entirely natural that Irish young adults should leave Ireland in search of *Lebensraum* or 'living space' abroad. This suggests that 'new wave' emigration is a welcome development because it encourages young adults to leave Ireland in search of work and opportunity abroad.

Despite the strong sense of place and of community in Irish life and Irish history, places as communities scarcely feature in contemporary justifications for Irish emigration. Instead they are reduced to marketplaces or abstract national plains. They rarely feature as places in their own right or as the bases of community life.[85] Similarly, the emigrant is conceptualised as a geographically mobile *homo economicus* logically moving between labour markets in the ceaseless search for economic opportunity. This *equilibrium* route to emigration ignores its social and political functions in Irish society and characterises as free choices decisions that are in fact structured in local, national and international contexts. In this literature the market signals differences in income between Ireland and overseas labour markets, indicates where opportunities are to be found, channels emigrants to overseas fields of opportunity and determines the volume and social composition of Irish emigration. Reflecting the neo-classical framework within which they have couched their arguments, economists and cost-benefit analysts in particular have portrayed Irish emigration as a *transfer mechanism* which resolves labour surpluses at home by directing surplus labourers abroad. They have also posited the decision to emigrate at the level of the individual and avoided any social class analysis of the internationalisation of Irish workers. They simply reduce emigration to strict economic causes and consequences and subject emigrants to the compelling logic of an iron law of labour transfer.[86]

BEHAVIOURALISM, REVISIONISM AND IRISH EMIGRATION

As we have already seen, revisionism has done much to exorcise the 'blame Britain' ethos from nationalist accounts of Irish social problems. Revisionism has also shaped attitudes to a wide range of contemporary issues, including unemployment, urban poverty and emigration. Indeed revisionism has marked a new intellectual watershed in the making of modern Ireland and Irish modernisation theory (the intellectual strategy used to explain social change in Ireland today). As such, it has occupied a central position in revisionist historiography and Irish political economy. It is not just that modernisation theory has become widely accepted as more 'politically correct' than traditional nationalist accounts of Irish history and Irish politics. In Ireland, revisionism and modernisation theory literally marked the coming of age of a new institutionalised and state-centred Irish intelligentsia who have sought to break from what they perceive as the 'narrow nationalism' of the nineteenth century by embracing the narrow logic of cost-benefit analysis. This intellectual project has 'sanitised' Irish social problems and the Irish historical record to such an extent that problems like emigration, poverty and unemployment hardly appear as *social* problems any more, let alone as *national* social problems. Adapting a 'blame the victim' approach which originated in the US to suit Irish conditions in the late '60s, they traced Irish social problems to the social psychological attitudes and attributes of individuals, and to the 'cultures' of poverty, emigration and unemployment within which these individuals function.

It is important to note that this new intellectual posture, although deeply ideological, was not the offshoot of 'conspiracy theory'. It developed from what Karl Mannheim has labelled 'the collective unconscious' of Irish society.[87] Since the '60s it has also shown every sign of valid scholarship, complete with copious scientific terminology and a new empiricism which sought to 'let the facts speak for themselves' rather than have nationalists interpret them to suit their agenda. Revisionism, including revised views of recent emigration, has held a position of such exclusive validity that disagreement with the new canons of revisionism has variously been considered unwise, unfashionable, radical, irresponsible and even unenlightened.

Revisionism also has so thoroughly pervaded our most crucial assumptions about Irish society that its effects have often gone unnoticed. This is particularly apparent in the case of Irish attitudes to emigration. Political leaders, and the general public, increasingly regard Europe and the United States as acceptable hosts to Ireland's surplus labour. In so doing they de-nationalise the causes of Irish emigration and externalise its solutions. The roots of this sanitised and voluntaristic perspective on emigration are traceable to the behaviouralism of the '60s. Behavioural and quantitative approaches to social issues then caused them to be analysed in great empirical detail to the neglect of theoretical explanation. Since then behaviouralists in particular have attributed migration and emigration from Ireland to the 'idiocy of rural life' and to the educational qualifications and social psychological attributes of Irish young adults. However there is every danger that the unopposed development of these behavioural and locational explanations may result in the causes of Irish emigration being traced simply to the presence or absence of an 'enterprising spirit' in Irish young adults or to Ireland's peripheral location in the European Union.

A WORLD-SYSTEMS PERSPECTIVE

Given its scale and composition it is clear that Irish emigration is not simply a voluntary activity which attracts the upwardly mobile. It is also an intrinsically geographical and social class phenomenon in that it had clear geographical causes and social consequences which in turn structured and were structured by the regions which emigrants left behind and by the regions where they settled.

However, contrary to modernisation and conventional core-periphery theories, emigration cannot be explained away with reference to simple locational categories like 'core' and 'periphery'. Neither can it be accounted for by 'push' and 'pull' factors operating between Ireland and the world economy or by the behavioural attributes of Irish young adults.

World-systems theory offers perspectives on the processes of emigration, migration, core formation and peripheralisation which are quite different from those of conventional geographical explanations. In particular it treats cores and peripheries as products of social and historical *processes* operating alongside developments in rural society, industry, transportation and technology. As Peter Taylor has argued, world-systems theorists use terms like 'core' and 'periphery':

> to refer to complex processes and not directly to areas, regions or states. The latter only become core-like because of a predominance of core processes operating in that particular area, region, or state. Similarly peripheral areas, regions or states are defined as those where peripheral processes dominate. This is not a trivial semantic point but directly relates to the way in which the spatial structure [of the world-economy] is structured.[88]

This is quite unlike the locational approach to core-periphery relations in conventional explanations of Irish emigration. These *activate* spatial categories and use them to explain away complex social processes. Thus 'cores', 'peripheries' and revolutions in transportation constitute explanations for emigration rather than simply facilitating it. In these circumstances 'cores' pull migrants to them, while 'peripheries' push emigrants from them. In world-systems theory, places, regions and urban centres have value in their own right. They are neither core nor periphery by locational nature. Instead they become such through the operation of historical geographical processes. As such they are the structuring and structured contexts wherein people make decisions about the changing world in which they live, including decisions about migration and emigration.

World-systems theory also shows how the expansion of capitalism in the nineteenth century encroached upon new societies and reoriented them to serve the wider needs of the world economy, not least by transforming some into emigrant nurseries for supplying industrial nations with cheap and adaptable labour. This frequently contributed to the peripheralisation of the former and the development of industrial cores in the latter. It also meant that peripheral societies did not join the world economy as 'equal partners' with industrial nations. They entered instead as the political and economic subordinates of the latter and were incorporated into the world economy on unfavourable terms.

World-systems theory is particularly suited to an analysis of Irish emigration and allows us to see it for what it always has been – a complex historical, geographical and social *process* which linked the peripheralisation of rural and urban Ireland to the emergence of core areas of native capitalism and the growth of industrial cores in the international economy. It also allows us to place Ireland in its proper international context and to show that, far from being marginal to the process of industrial development and colonial expansion, emigration rendered Ireland central to the process of core formation in the world economy. Revolutions in transportation have simply facilitated, but by no means caused, the internationalisation of Irish labour since the nineteenth century. They also forced even the most isolated pockets of rural Ireland into the world economy. Thus the annihilation of spatial barriers to the circulation of agricultural produce and labour simultaneously transformed Ireland into a functioning unit within the world economy while transforming it also into an emigrant nursery.

Like many Third World countries today, post-Famine Ireland was transformed into an export-led economy highly susceptible to price fluctuations and to changes in overseas demand for agricultural exports and labour. This has contributed to the commodification and internationalisation of Irish labour and continuously causes new values to be placed on rural and working-class communities. To argue thus is not to suggest that Ireland has naturally been a labour surplus economy. It is merely to suggest that the forms of economic development adopted by dominant sectors in Irish society since the nineteenth century have generated surpluses of specific types of labour and caused emigration to be treated as an acceptable solution for disposing of Mother Ireland's surplus sons and daughters. Criticising the designation of Ireland as a 'labour-surplus economy' Ó Tuathaigh has also argued that this:

> is a highly relativistic and . . . treacherous term. . . . What is 'surplus' is only to be considered surplus in the context of a specific social and economic order, a specific system of economic development and social formation, a specific set of ideas, values, priorities and policies dominant within any given society. Indeed, it was precisely this understanding of the totality of factors impinging on the demographic/emigration pattern in Ireland that informed the nationalist critique of emigration in the period of the Union. As Ireland was a neglected, exploited, peripheral part of the British state, it suffered loss of population. If it were the core concern of a native Irish government, its economic development would be a priority, its capacity to retain and maintain a much larger population unquestionable. The logic of the nationalist case would be that Ireland was a 'labour-surplus economy' only in the context of its subordinate and exploited status within the British state.[89]

However, in tracing Ireland's status as a 'surplus labour economy' to the fact that it was 'a peripheral part of the British state', Ó Tuathaigh falls for a familiar geographical explanation of Irish emigration. In tracing emigration to the *British* connection — 'absentee landlords, draining off of rents, underinvestment, no development alternatives to a single market' — he Anglicises the causes and nationalises the solutions to Irish emigration.[90] He particularly ignores the roots of emigration in Irish property relations and in Ireland's peripheral status in the modern world system.

5. 'NEW WAVE' EMIGRATION: THE MODERNISATION OF IRISH EMIGRATION?

WHAT'S 'NEW' ABOUT 'NEW WAVE' EMIGRATION?

Given the volume of recent emigration and its structuring role in Irish society, it is surprising that it has been so 'sanitised' and 'individualised' by its new apologists. The exodus has been estimated at an annual average of 14,400 between 1981 and 1986, rising to 28,000 in 1986 and an average of 51,000 per annum between 1987 and 1988.[91] Since the '80s, emigration is particularly affecting Irish teenagers. A recent sample survey by the Department of Labour found that 1,800 school-leavers out of a total of 60,900 surveyed had emigrated within one year of leaving school.[92] Courtney has suggested that total emigration between April 1982 and April 1988 was 224,000.[93] Another estimate suggests that 289,000 emigrants left Ireland between 1982 and 1983. These figures exclude the large number of illegal Irish immigrants in the United States, where the Irish Emigration Reform Movement recently estimated 'illegals' at approximately 135,000 upwards of

20,000 in Boston alone.[94] Estimates of the number of 'illegal Irish' in New York city vary from a low of 40,000 to a high of over 100,000.[95] The number of emigrants leaving the country is much smaller than the pool of potential emigrants. Thus for example 120,000 Irish people applied for visas to enter Australia in 1986 but only 1,251 were successful.[96]

Given these levels of emigration it is not surprising that one journalist could recently argue that 'the exodus of young people in the past decade has so depopulated parts of the west of Ireland that parish priests in rural Mayo and Galway can't put together a dance'.[97] Another commentator has suggested that many Irish people in their twenties today regard Christmas as 'the only time of the year when one half of their generation meets the other'.[98] These statements show how easy it is to fall for the stereotyped image of Irish emigration as a rural phenomenon. 'New wave' Irish emigration, like the nineteenth-century exodus, is a mixture of urban and rural emigration. Courtney has shown that Dublin, Cork, Galway, Limerick and Waterford all experienced net emigration between 1981 and 1986.[99]

Table 5.1: Gross migratory outflow in 1987/88 classified by the social group of the household head in which the emigrant previously resided.

Social Group	Rate per 1000 population		
	Males	Females	Persons
Farmers	12.4	12.4	12.4
Professionals	19.3	14.4	16.8
Employers/Managers	19.9	16.2	18.1
Salaried intermediate non-manual	15.3	13.4	14.3
Other non-manual	21.3	14.5	18.0
Skilled, Semi-skilled manual	18.9	12.1	15.6
Unskilled	19.1	10.6	15.2
Unknown	48.8	9.3	22.4
Total	**19.1**	**12.8**	**15.9**

Source: Labour Survey (1988).

Results from most recent surveys of Irish emigration suggest that 'new wave' emigration is still largely a survival strategy for working-class and small-farming families which is increasingly affecting middle-class families. They also suggest that large numbers of young adults take to the 'emigrant trail' at an early age. Thus the National Economic and Social Council (NESC) survey found that the majority of recent emigrants were aged between fifteen and twenty-four years when they left the country. It also found that second-level school-leavers still account for the majority of emigrants. This suggests that the traditional view of the Irish emigrant as unskilled manual workers, or possessing only rudimentary skills, must be revised to include large numbers of emigrants with second- and third-level qualifications.[100] Certainly large numbers of Irish emigrants now possess qualifications from third level colleges and universities and this more than anything else sets them apart from many of their nineteenth-century counterparts, although it is important to note these also included middle-class emigrants. The NESC survey found that twenty-six per cent of the 11,300 third-level award recipients who left full-time education in 1988 had emigrated by the following spring. It also raised important questions about the effects of emigration on Irish society and questioned the manner in which higher education in Ireland is subsidised from general taxation while the benefits of that education often accrue to Britain or other European countries. Thus it has been increasingly suggested that the criteria for funding existing third-level courses in Ireland from EU revenue should be extended to include engineering and a wide range of other courses. Until this happens, it could be argued, the 'brain drain' component in Irish emigration will contribute to the peripheralisation of Ireland. This will represent a significant loss not only in terms of resources invested in education but also in social and political terms. In leaving the country, young adults are contributing to the senilisation of rural and urban communities and may well be consolidating the hegemonic status of conservative and right-of-centre parties.

Table 5.2 Estimated gross migration outflow from Ireland to year ending April 1988. Classified by sex and age.

Age	(000s)			(%)		
	Male	Female	Total	Male	Female	Total
0–14	0.5	0.5	1.0	1.5	2.2	1.8
15–24	22.0	16.8	38.8	65.3	74.0	68.8
25–44	10.3	5.0	15.3	30.6	22.0	27.1
45–64	0.9	0.3	1.2	2.6	1.3	2.1
65 +	–	0.1	0.1	–	0.4	0.2
Totals	**33.7**	**22.6**	**56.4**	**100.0**	**100.0**	**100.0**

Source: Labour Force Survey (1988).

Table 5.3: Proportion of 1988 third-level award recipients who emigrated according to type of qualification.

Qualification	%
Primary Degree	36
Higher Degree	27
H. Dip. in Education	27
B. Education	6
Sub-Degrees	25
All Qualifications	**29**

Source: NESC Report (1992).

SOCIAL CHARACTERISTICS OF RECENT EMIGRANTS

To establish the social characteristics and destinations of recent emigrants the author of this study conducted questionnaire surveys in a number of urban and rural settings in the south and west of Ireland. The survey (henceforth referred to as the West of Ireland Survey) was conducted between February and June, 1989. It targeted just over 6,000 families with a total population of almost

17,000 young adults aged sixteen years or older and obtained information on the social characteristics of just under 2,200 emigrants (See also appendices A and B). Post-intermediate students in secondary schools acted as surrogates for their parents in this survey and constituted an important source of data on the social characteristics and destinations of family members who had recently emigrated. The methodology of the survey was partially influenced by local demand for information on the social characteristics of young emigrants. With the exception of Cork city, information about emigrants was obtained from all schools in each survey area. However places in this survey are not to be considered as 'case studies' for illustrating local variations of a national theme. They are places in their own right as well as being the local worlds where the respondents lived and the communities from which many of their brothers and sisters had recently emigrated. Statisticians and demographers who occupy the national plain usually ignore such local worlds. In so doing they often underestimate the localised causes and consequences of contemporary emigration.

There were three advantages to the place-centred approach of this survey. Firstly, it 'empowered' local communities with information about emigration from their areas.[101] Secondly, it targeted an important source of recent emigration in concentrating on families with children still in second- or third-level education, including those with children who had recently emigrated. Thirdly, it showed that local activists and community organisations need not await national surveys to obtain detailed information at community level. Indeed this survey suggests that with standardisation of methodology and synchronisation of data collection, local communities can engage in the comparative study of emigration at local, regional and community levels. These are the levels at which most people live. As Agnew (1989) and Lovering (1984) have shown, social scientists through their participation in such projects, can strengthen democracy by empowering communities and providing grassroots movements with data about national issues at local level. To argue thus is not to suggest the total abandonment of national surveys in favour of local analysis – it is merely to emphasise that places matter to students of emigration as well as emigrants, and that the proper starting points for studying emigration are the local worlds of those most affected by it, not the abstract national plains inhabited by statisticians, demographers and economists.

There were a number of limitations to this survey which emphasised the need to supplement it with results from the NESC survey of the social and economic implications of recent emigration. Firstly, although it established the social characteristics of emigrants from an important source of recent emigration, namely families with young adults of emigrant age, the targeted population was not a statistical sample. Thus it did not allow for the construction of regional or national patterns of emigration through an analysis of local trends. Secondly, some sections of the local population were excluded and this limits its utility as a regional census. These included established families spanning several decades of emigration history who had no one in post-intermediate education at the time of the survey. It also included early school-leavers who may have emigrated before entering post-intermediate classes and who had no brothers or sisters in these classes. It finally excluded families that may have emigrated as a unit, and those living locally who sent their children elsewhere to be educated.

One-fifth of the 6,018 families in the West of Ireland Survey had at least one member living abroad. This suggests that many families in Ireland may be classified as 'transnational households' because so many have family members working abroad.[102] Thirteen per cent of 'emigrant families' had three or more emigrants.

The West of Ireland Survey also found that the popular portrayal of emigration as 'a blight on Irish society' is neither socially nor geographically accurate. Emigration is still more deeply embedded

Table 5.4: Targeted population and emigrant families per survey area.

Survey Area	Number of families	Number of emigrant families	Emigrants as % total
Cork City	1,720	341	19.8
Limerick City	891	176	19.7
Tralee	690	174	25.5
South Galway	641	127	19.8
Skibbereen	437	109	24.9
Waterford	429	86	20.1
Inishowen	321	65	20.2
Schull/Ballydehob	219	57	26.0
Cloughaneely	217	54	24.9
Wexford	210	43	20.5
South Limerick	179	34	19.0
Raphoe	64	13	20.3
Totals	**6,018**	**1,279**	**21.3**

Source: West of Ireland Survey.

in small-farming and working-class communities than in middle-class suburbs, although these are also being affected by emigration, including involuntary emigration. Provincial cities and county towns all over Ireland are once again functioning as 'emigrant nurseries'. However, contrary to King and Shuttleworth, the urban bias in 'new-wave' emigration is not simply a reflection of the urbanisation of the Irish population.[103] Instead it is due to the deterioration of urban labour markets and to the lack of jobs and promotional opportunities in Irish urban centres.[104]

The West of Ireland Survey also suggests that the sanitised image of emigrants as individuals possessing impressive qualifications needs to be revised if we are to take account of the large number of young emigrants who take to the emigrant trail before completing their secondary education. It also found that emigrants with second-level qualifications accounted for just over two-thirds of all emigrants.

These results are in keeping with other surveys on the age structure and educational levels of recent Irish emigrants. Thus a Department of Labour survey of 1987 school-leavers found that just over seven per cent had emigrated within a year of leaving school. Another survey conducted by the Action Group for Irish Youth in London found that almost one-quarter of those interviewed had left school without taking any examinations. Finally, in a survey of emigration from Cork city in 1988 one-quarter of emigrants had completed their secondary education up to junior certificate level, thirty-nine per cent had a leaving certificate, eleven per cent were university degree holders and over twelve per cent had completed a third-level diploma course.[105] For many Irish young adults it would appear that Ireland and England not only constitute a 'single market for

Table 5.5: Educational qualifications of emigrants
(percentage of emigrants to UK only).

Study area	Inter./Group Cert.	Leaving Cert.	Third Level	Total Emigrants
	%	%	%	
Cloughaneely	50.6	34.9	14.5	83
Schull/Ballydehob	37.1	43.5	19.4	62
Inishowen	34.7	42.4	22.9	118
Limerick	27.4	49.2	23.4	197
South Limerick	23.8	52.4	23.8	42
Waterford	21.2	53.8	25.0	132
Tralee	20.7	45.4	33.9	174
South Galway	20.5	54.1	25.4	161
Wexford	18.4	58.3	23.3	60
Skibbereen	18.2	45.4	36.4	143
Cork City	14.8	46.4	38.8	325
Raphoe	0.0	69.6	30.4	23
Totals	**23.2**	**48.0**	**28.8**	**1,520**

Source: West of Ireland Survey

cultural consumption' but also a single labour market.[106] Contrary to conventional wisdom, this does not mean that the trauma of emigration is less today than it was in the nineteenth century.

Given the age structure and qualifications of recent emigrants, it is difficult to account for the popular view of 'new wave' emigration as an upwardly mobile activity chiefly attracting high achievers. The NESC survey found that almost seventy per cent of the estimated 56,500 emigrants who left Ireland in the year ending April 1988 were aged between fifteen and twenty-four years. A higher proportion of females (74 per cent) than males (65 per cent) were in the fifteen to twenty-four age-group category. One-third of all emigrants in the West of Ireland Survey, and forty per cent of those who went to Britain, were teenagers when they left home. Thus, unlike their peers in the core areas of the European Union, adolescents in Ireland, particularly those in remote rural areas, are frequently subject to the trauma of emigration at an early age.

IRELAND'S MULTINATIONAL FAMILIES

We have already seen that much nineteenth-century Irish emigration was a strategy for family survival which enabled poor families to shed 'surplus' sons and daughters and thereby conserve scarce family resources. Emigration also affects the families and communities that emigrants leave behind.[107] Although the social psychological effects of emigration on families were beyond the scope of the West of Ireland Survey, it did allow for a crude evaluation of the embeddedness of emigration in urban and rural communities. One-fifth of the families in this survey had at least one member living abroad. Thirteen per cent of 'emigrant families' had three or more emigrants and six per cent had four or more emigrants (Tables 5.6 and 5.8). The 'embeddedness' of emigration is particularly noticeable in the case of the north-west of Ireland where one in four families in parts of Donegal had at least one member living

Table 5.6: Number of emigrants per emigrant family.

Survey Area	Number of families	Number of emigrants			
		1	2	3	≥4
		%	%	%	%
Cork City	341	65.1	25.3	6.1	3.5
Limerick	176	63.3	21.4	7.2	8.1
Tralee	174	67.2	20.6	7.4	4.8
South Galway	127	64.7	25.3	4.7	5.3
Skibbereen	109	60.3	21.4	7.2	8.1
Waterford	86	61.8	22.0	8.0	7.2
Inishowen	65	57.1	21.2	10.3	11.4
Schull/Ballydehob	57	59.9	21.4	11.2	6.5
Cloghaneely	54	56.3	20.1	11.7	11.9
Wexford	43	70.1	23.6	5.8	0.5
South Limerick	34	70.4	23.1	5.1	1.4
Raphoe	13	70.3	20.4	7.3	2.0
Totals	**1,279**	**63.8**	**22.1**	**7.8**	**5.8**

Source: West of Ireland Survey.

abroad. Emigrant families were one-quarter of all families in parts of Kerry where almost twelve per cent of emigrant families had three or more members living or working abroad. However, contrary to another piece of conventional wisdom, emigration in Ireland today is not *caused* by large families. Ever since the nineteenth century, families in Ireland have been transformed to suit the changing needs of dominant social classes and to supply the core areas of the world economy with cheap and adaptable labour. The transnational nature of the Irish family has also long been intimately bound up with the changing circumstances of Irish capitalism. This paradox in Irish political and economic life – the scattering of the sons and daughters of 'Mother Ireland' abroad in the interests of fostering a *specific type* of economic growth and political culture back home – has created a profound contradiction at the very heart of Irish politics. It has also meant that nationalism in contemporary Ireland has operated quite differently from nationalism in other European countries. Benedict Anderson has pointed out that the language of nationalism singles out women and the home as the symbolic repositories of group identity and describes its object using either the vocabulary of kinship, motherland and fatherland, or home, *Heimat*.[108] It does this in order to denote something to which one is 'naturally' tied. In the case of late-nineteenth and early twentieth-century Ireland, nationalism served this important 'territorialising' function for dominant sectors of Irish society at least. However, the radical devaluation of nationalism in Ireland means that here, unlike in France, Germany, Britain and Scandinavia, the 'territorialising' or *anchoring* role of nationalism has never applied to all of 'Mother Ireland's' sons and daughters, many of whom still have to seek *lebensraum* abroad.

The Irish family has long been loaded with a double burden as a result of emigration. On the one hand it has acted as the social terrain of personal life, a private space where mother, father and children are expected to share a healthy emotional and material life. Thus the family in colonial Ireland was expected to fulfil the same functions as it did in mature industrial nations like Britain and the United States. On the other hand, families here were not only social arenas where the inner emotional life of the family met with the full force of the external economy – they were also places where the structuring forces of national and international capitalism intersected and helped to push young adults onto the emigrant trail at an early age.[109] Thus in Ireland the twin forces of capitalism and emigration have had a powerful *structuring* effect upon the social composition of Irish families, and upon rural, working-class and middle-class communities. This in turn has added to the contradictions surrounding the Irish family.

Ever since its institutionalisation in article 41.2 of the 1937 constitution, the traditional Irish patriarchal family was meant to act as an emotional retreat and a cocoon which protected its members from the *ennui* of social and economic life outside the family and outside Ireland. The degree of opposition to any amendments to family law as articulated in that constitution shows the extent to which certain sectors in Irish society at least wish to go on treating the Irish family as though it can be cosseted against the external world, including legislative reform originating outside Ireland. However, while church and state teach reverence for family values and respect for the sanctity of human life, political and social leaders since the nineteenth century have condoned emigration as a solution to Irish economic problems. Thus the sanctity of the family as enshrined in the 1937 constitution is in stark contrast with a reality which sees emigration, often of quite young teenagers, embedded in the economic landscape and political system of this country. Moreover, in the very parts of this country where support for the traditional family, and opposition to divorce, abortion and family planning is strongest, teenagers of eighteen years and under can account for up to one-third of total emigration.

Emigration not only affects family life but clearly also affects the social structure of urban and rural communities and transforms country towns into 'dormitory towns'.[110] Indeed large numbers of smaller towns and villages in rural Ireland today are in danger of 'dying' in much the same way that island communities have 'died' through the 'senilisation' of their communities since the nineteenth century.[111] This aspect of community decay – the death of balanced communities through emigration and senilisation – is also evident in rural Ireland today where entire communities are fading away due to the senilisation of their population and the emigration of their youth. Thus for example in 1986 one small town in north Mayo lost no less than 300 young adults through emigration in a single year, and seventy-five per cent of these were moving to the US, where many were 'illegals'.[112] Provincial cities and county towns are also witnessing the re-opening of emigrant trails that were temporarily closed during the 'boom' years of the '60s and '70s and this will undoubtedly affect their demographic structure.

DESTINATIONS OF 'NEW WAVE' EMIGRANTS

Recent Irish emigrants may be entering 'virgin territory' for Irish emigrants by moving to mainland Europe, Japan and many Third World countries. However, despite official perceptions of 'new wave' emigration as a European phenomenon, Britain still accounts for the majority of Irish emigrants (Table 5.7). The West of Ireland Survey found that Britain still accounts for approximately two-thirds of all recent Irish emigrants. The NESC survey also found that just under seventy per cent of all those who left the state in the year ending April 1988 went to the UK. The United States accounted for almost fourteen per cent of all emigrants in

Table 5.7: Destinations of emigrants.

Survey area	London	Other UK	North America	EU	Other	Total
Cloughaneely	59.0	24.0	11.0	2.0	4.0	100
Wexford	58.3	13.2	11.9	7.1	9.5	84
Tralee	58.0	13.1	18.3	3.3	7.3	245
Raphoe	57.7	30.9	3.8	3.8	3.8	26
South Galway	56.8	11.4	22.9	3.0	5.9	236
Inishowen	56.7	18.5	15.9	1.3	7.6	157
Skibbereen	56.2	17.5	15.3	6.7	4.1	194
Limerick	51.7	16.2	16.6	4.8	10.7	290
Waterford	51.4	15.2	15.6	6.7	11.1	198
Cork	46.0	17.6	18.4	11.3	7.6	511
Schull/Ballydehob	45.2	28.6	21.4	1.2	3.6	84
South Limerick	42.2	23.4	18.7	1.6	14.1	64
Totals	**52.5**	**16.9**	**17.3**	**5.5**	**7.8**	**2,189**

Source: West of Ireland Survey.

that year. Both surveys suggest that Irish young adults may now perceive London, not Dublin, as 'their' capital. They may also see it in much the same light as their peers from the north of England and Scotland see it – a field of opportunity for those capable of adapting to the needs of the labour market and an easy place from which to return home often.

The geography of recent Irish emigration to Britain has also altered significantly in recent years and far fewer emigrants are going to the midlands or the north of England and lowland Scotland than previously. This is particularly true of emigration from the west and north-west of Ireland, which have regularly served as 'emigrant nurseries', supplying the industrial and agricultural heartlands of Scotland and northern England with cheap labour. The findings of the West of Ireland Survey support Bronwen Walter's contention that the vast majority of 'new wave' emigration to Britain is going to London and the south-east.[113] Indeed the volume of Irish youth emigration to London may be facilitating further emigration and exacerbating problems confronting young Irish people there. The latter provide information and support for those back home who may be contemplating a move to London but the volume of emigration to the city may be heightening competition among young Irish emigrants in their search for low-paid jobs and cheap accommodation.

Given the volume of recent emigration, it is difficult to understand how the gentrified image of the modern Irish emigrant as an upwardly mobile individual has survived. Table 5.8 suggests that those projecting this image overestimate the preparedness of young adults for emigration. They also exaggerate the *voluntary* nature of emigration. The findings of the West of Ireland and the NESC surveys therefore suggest that recent emigrants are not that different from those who stay at home. Their educational and other qualifications are best evaluated in terms of contemporary labour market needs, rather than focusing on the undoubted gaps that separate today's emigrants from their predecessors. Certainly the age structure of emigrants in both the NESC survey and in the West of Ireland Survey seriously challenges the official 'sanitised' image of recent emigration. However it must be emphasised that the method for establishing the age structure and qualifications of emigrants in the West of Ireland Survey was necessarily simple and consequently is open to criticism. Respondents were simply asked the age and qualifications of family members who had emigrated. More detailed analysis is necessary to assess the educational selectivity of emigrants by comparing them with non-emigrants.

Table 5.8: Emigrant age at leaving home
(Percentage of emigrants to UK only).

Study Area	<18	18	19	20	21	≥22
Cloughaneely	15.7	20.5	12.1	12.1	16.8	22.8
Wexford	13.3	18.4	15.0	13.3	16.7	23.3
Schull/Ballydehob	12.9	14.5	12.9	16.1	11.3	32.3
Waterford	11.4	17.4	18.9	15.9	9.1	27.3
South Galway	11.2	14.8	21.1	13.7	11.2	28.0
Limerick	10.7	16.2	16.6	14.2	7.6	34.5
Skibbereen	10.5	11.2	9.1	12.6	17.4	39.2
South Limerick	9.5	9.5	28.6	7.1	7.1	38.2
Inishowen	9.3	26.3	12.7	16.9	11.1	23.7
Tralee	6.9	11.5	16.1	12.1	16.6	36.8
Cork City	4.6	9.2	15.2	12.9	13.5	44.6
Raphoe	4.3	21.7	21.7	4.3	17.4	30.6
Totals	**9.3**	**14.6**	**15.8**	**13.4**	**12.8**	**34.1**

Source: West of Ireland Survey.

However, if age is considered one indicator of the 'preparedness' of young adults for the emigrant trail, the NESC and the West of Ireland surveys suggest that too many are emigrating too young. This is particularly true of areas of high unemployment where young adults are leaving before completing their secondary schooling. Forty per cent of emigrants in the West of Ireland Survey who went to Britain left home before they were twenty years old. Two-thirds left before they were twenty-two years old. Those leaving urban areas are probably leaving older than their rural counterparts and this may be particularly true of young female emigrants. Thus in the West of Ireland Survey, forty per cent of urban emigrants to Britain were twenty-two years or more when they left the country. The corresponding figure for rural emigrants was just over thirty per cent. Thirty-four per cent of the Cork and Limerick emigrants who went to Britain were under twenty when they left home. The corresponding figure for all other areas was almost forty-three per cent. Again both surveys support the contention that the teenage years for many Irish young adults are years of considerable stress, to which emigration contributes. Stress induced through competitive examinations at school is often followed by the stressful experiences of emigration. In the West of Ireland Survey seventeen per cent of urban, and twenty-six per cent of rural emigrants to Britain were eighteen years or less when they left home. The corresponding figures for female emigrants were twenty and twenty-eight per cent respectively. In a survey carried out in London in 1986 it was found that fifty-seven per cent of recent Irish emigrants had made no prior accommodation arrangements before leaving Ireland. Seventeen per cent of the total slept rough on their first nights in the city, thirty-four per cent had less than £30 and seventy per cent had less than £100 when they arrived in the city.[114]

While those emigrating to mainland Europe and the United States are generally older than Irish emigrants to Britain, the West of Ireland Survey found that one-quarter of emigrants to the US and one-third of those who moved to mainland Europe were under twenty when they left home. Certainly younger emigrants tended to have lower educational qualifications than older emigrants, and young women may be leaving somewhat better qualified than males. The West of Ireland Survey found few discrepancies in the qualifications of those entering the US compared to those emigrating to Britain. Indeed Irish emigrants to mainland Europe are among the best-qualified of recent Irish emigrants and almost half of them had a third-level qualification. One recent survey of the 'Parisian Irish' found that seventy-six per cent had a secondary education, thirty-five per cent had a teaching qualification, and seventy per cent of male and fifty-one per cent of females had a university education.[115] Both the NESC report and the West of Ireland Survey suggest that those leaving large cities may be better qualified than their small-town and rural counterparts. In the West of Ireland Survey one-third of emigrants from Cork and Limerick had a third-level qualification and the corresponding figure for all areas excluding these two urban areas was twenty-seven per cent. While such 'high achievers' and graduate emigrants have certainly added a qualitative dimension to recent Irish emigration, it is hardly significant enough to talk of its 'gentrification'. Highly-qualified university graduates tend to attract more media attention than graduate emigrants from technical colleges in Ireland, despite the fact that this latter group probably outnumbers university graduates on the emigrant trails out of Ireland. In emigrant blackspots like Donegal, Kerry and Mayo those with third-level qualifications probably account for less than one-fifth of total emigrants and the majority of these are not university graduates. Regional colleges, originally established to raise the quality of young adults entering the Irish labour market, have recently been witnessing a large number of their graduates leaving Ireland. Many of these may be over-qualified for the jobs that they acquire in cities as far apart as San Francisco and Berlin. They are also filling gaps in the supply of unskilled and semi-skilled labour in overseas labour markets. Moreover, many of those with secondary or third-level qualifications may belong to a 'wait-and-see' group of potential emigrants – young adults who stay in second- or third-level colleges in order to prolong the date of emigrating or to better qualify themselves to work abroad. This may be particularly true of those living in and around urban centres with access to third-level colleges. Others in this 'wait-and-see' group may have emigrated after a spell on the 'dole', or an unsuccessful spell of job-hunting on the home market.[116] Reductions in the relative costs of travel are probably reducing the immediate costs of emigrating from rural areas and provincial towns throughout Ireland. While this does not 'cause' emigration as conventional wisdom suggests, it may encourage Irish young adults to think only of travel costs, and to ignore the other costs of emigrating.

NEW 'SEASONAL MIGRANTS'?

Young Irish emigrants are returning so frequently that we may now be witnessing a new form of 'seasonal migration' in Ireland. Today's emigrants return to Ireland during seasonal holidays, and this more than anything else sets them apart from their nineteenth and early-twentieth century predecessors. In the late '80s the majority of emigrants returned home on holiday at least once a year. Thus young adults who work in England, particularly those in the London area, often return home on 'seasonal' holidays and this is reflected in the increased profits of airlines and ferry services, and in the increased volume of sea and air traffic between Britain and Ireland at Christmas time, Easter and during the summer. The West of Ireland Survey found that almost one-third of the emigrants to Britain had been home three times or more in the twelve months before the survey was conducted. Fifteen per cent had been home four times or more. However, fifteen per cent of those who emigrated to Britain had not been home once in the twelve-month period. Frequency of return home on holiday may indicate an easing of the trauma of emigration, but it may equally point to the involuntary nature of much recent emigration. More detailed analysis of emigrant attitudes to home and host countries is needed before we can establish this. We particularly need to know if young emigrants in casual or unskilled work 'hoard' holidays or shift between jobs in order to spend time at home. The fact that they return so often is an indication of the strong family and peer links that young Irish emigrants still retain with home.

Table 5.9: Frequency of return home in one 12-month period (emigrants to UK only).

| Survey area | Number of times returned home | | | | | Total emigrants |
	0	1	2	3	≥4	
South Limerick	21.4	33.3	16.7	21.4	7.2	42
Skibbereen	21.0	18.8	26.6	18.2	15.4	143
Waterford	20.5	25.8	26.5	12.8	14.4	132
Cork	18.8	23.1	23.1	15.6	19.4	325
Limerick	15.7	26.9	25.9	12.2	19.3	197
South Galway	14.3	27.3	32.9	13.7	11.8	161
Wexford	13.3	28.3	38.3	8.3	11.8	60
Schull/Ballydehob	12.9	30.6	25.8	17.8	12.9	62
Tralee	12.1	23.0	32.2	21.2	11.5	174
Cloughaneely	12.1	23.0	33.7	22.8	8.4	83
Inishowen	9.3	21.2	25.4	23.8	20.3	118
Raphoe	4.3	13.1	26.1	26.1	30.4	23
Totals	**15.8**	**24.2**	**27.6**	**16.8**	**15.6**	**1,520**

Source: West of Ireland Survey.

Recent emigrants are undoubtedly spending money saved abroad on frequent and expensive trips home. For this reason also they differ from their late-nineteenth and early-twentieth century predecessors whose emigrant 'remittances' supplemented the incomes of large working-class and poor rural families. For many of those in marginal occupations, particularly those in the 'black economy' in the United States, the trip home may be too expensive or too risky. Many of the 379 emigrants to the US and Canada targeted in the West of Ireland Survey may be in 'emigrant traps' – having entered the United States, they may be afraid to return home on holiday because of the high risk of detection by US immigration authorities.

Emigrants with professional qualifications undoubtedly constitute an 'emigrant aristocracy' in this survey (Appendices 1 and 2). Members of this are certainly higher on the social ladder and are probably more widely scattered throughout the international labour market than emigrants from working-class and poor-farming backgrounds. The pinnacle of the male emigrant aristocracy is still occupied by engineers, dentists, doctors, accountants and other professionals. This group accounted for sixteen per cent of male emigrants in the West of Ireland Survey. The professions accounted for significantly more male than female emigrants. However, although many of the Irish who moved to Britain in the '60s and '70s did well and were assimilated into British society, their cultural identity has either been unrecognised or unacceptable.[117] This makes life especially difficult for 'failed emigrants' who do not find work or job security abroad. Below the pinnacles of emigrant professional employment the majority of male and female emigrants lead humbler lives and occupy the traditional occupations of the emigrant. One survey in the early '80s found that seventy-six per cent of Irish men in Britain were manual workers, compared with eighty per cent for Afro-Caribbean and forty-nine per cent for white British-born males.[118] Male emigrants still gravitate to the construction industry which accounted for forty per cent of male emigrants in the West of Ireland Survey. There may also be significant regional variations in the degree of dependency on this industry, with disadvantaged rural areas and working-class districts supplying a disproportionate share of casual and unskilled labour. The West of Ireland Survey found that the construction industry accounted for more than two-thirds of male emigrants from north Donegal, west Cork and south Kerry. The corresponding figure for Cork city and Limerick was less than one-third. This suggests that large numbers of male emigrants are still filling gaps in the semi-skilled, unskilled and casual labour market. It also suggests that while a minority of Irish male emigrants are climbing social ladders abroad, many more are still climbing ladders.

IRISH WOMEN'S EXPERIENCE

As this study has consistently shown, popular perceptions of Irish emigrants are poor foundations for understanding recent or historical patterns of emigration. Popular perceptions have also created sexist stereotypes of emigrants as males, usually working-class males and in the construction industry or in roadworks.[119] Sexism still distorts popular images of Irish emigration today by writing off Irish women from the emigrant trails.[120] With a small number of notable exceptions, the history of Irish emigration has been written as though women did not matter. However, as Meenan has shown, women have outnumbered male emigrants for at least three decades between 1891 and 1961.[121] Indeed, the exodus of large numbers of young women often created serious sex imbalances in rural communities and it is still a matter of debate whether or not this has affected the mental well being of rural communities.[122] Despite their neglect in most recent accounts, women still account for almost half of all emigrants since the '80s. The NESC survey found that females accounted for almost forty per cent of those between fifteen and forty-four years who left Ireland in the year ending April, 1988. Forty-seven per cent of emigrants in the West of Ireland Survey were young women, many of them teenagers. These are among the most neglected sector in recent Irish emigration.

We have also seen that Irish women who emigrated in the late-nineteenth century were strongly represented in farm work, domestic service and factory work.[123] However, we witnessed some notable developments in patterns of Irish female emigration in recent decades, many of which were the result of war-induced labour shortages or developments in the welfare state and in part-time employment. Large numbers of those who emigrated to

Britain after World War II entered lower-middle-class positions in the welfare state. Still today Irish women emigrants who moved to London have ended up at a lower status than their non-immigrant peers, though many have been better off than if they had remained at home. [124]

A recent study of the causes and effects of emigration on Irish women argued that:

> The vast majority of women emigrate for employment-related reasons. Unemployment, lack of sufficient career opportunities and low paid, dead-end jobs in Ireland, *combined with labour shortages in Britain and elsewhere* and direct recruitment by these countries, provide the reasons for most emigration. Having said all that, women in particular have also emigrated because of what we may call 'social reasons', e.g. to escape domestic violence by travelling to Women's Aid shelters in England, to have an abortion, to conceal a pregnancy, to escape a feeling of not 'fitting in' because of beliefs or sexuality. [125] (Emphasis added).

Stressing the specificity of the female emigrant's experience since the mid-'80s these authors found that:

> Many women . . . have decided that they must get out of Ireland permanently and set up home somewhere else. Their main reason for leaving was the repressive moral and social climate in Ireland. They describe how narrow social attitudes and restrictive laws which had an impact on almost every aspect of their lives contributed to their decision to leave. Many told us that for them the defeat of the 1986 referendum on divorce symbolised the intolerant nature of Irish society and drove them to emigrate . . . women emigrants repeatedly stress that the inability of Irish society to tolerate dissent or disagreement and to acknowledge difference were major factors influencing their decision to leave. [126]

As Kelly and Nic Ghoille Coille have emphasised, the feminisation of overseas labour markets, especially in the UK and the United States, has also drawn Irish women abroad. Many of these have been only partially integrated into their host societies and occupy the lowest rungs of the labour market. Indeed, despite their numerical strength, Irish women are hidden from the history of recent Irish emigration largely because so many of them are scattered across a wide range of low income and 'invisible' employment. This category includes women working in neo-domestic-service occupations like hospital orderlies, au pair work and the catering trade. This contributes to the stereotyping of Irish emigration as a *male* activity and ignores the important functions of Irish female immigrants in the core areas of the world economy. Thus for example Bronwen Walter has recently argued:

> Irish women in London are doubly invisible in London.
> As members of an ethnic minority whose existence is
> frequently unrecognised and as women whose work is
> scattered in various homes, hospitals and offices their
> contribution to London's economic and social life is
> largely ignored. Yet they comprise ten per cent of all
> women in London. Their employment in particular
> sectors, notably nursing, catering and cleaning . . .
> *virtually underpins the day to day functioning of the city*.[127]
> (Emphasis added).

The fact that Irish communities abroad are male dominated in turn means that Irish women emigrants have fewer support networks than their male counterparts. This means that women emigrants experience difficulties in finding employment different to those of men, many of whom can rely on Irish contractors or other Irish employers of male labour to ease their entry into the labour force. As Kelly and Nic Ghoille Coille point out:

> The pressures on women to adapt and assimilate have
> always been stronger than on men because women

have always been more actively engaged in the
cultures in which they have lived.[128]

It has also been found that women's role as primary carers of children
adds to the pressure experienced by women emigrants and often
forces them to face decisions not only about their own ethnic
identity, but also that of their children, many of whom may be
brought up in multi-ethnic communities and in racially-mixed
families. This strain is particularly strong in Irish communities in
London where women feel extra pressure due to the fact that
many wish to make their children relate positively to their roots.

The West of Ireland Survey also found that like their post-war
counterparts young Irish women today are still scattered across a
wide range of occupations in the countries where they have settled.
These include neo-domestic service (e.g. cleaning workers, au
pairs and waitresses), lower-middle class occupations and
professional employment (See Appendix 2 for a more detailed
distribution of female emigrants in the late '80s). Thirty-eight per
cent of female emigrants in this survey left the country before they
were twenty years old. One-tenth had only primary or
intermediate education. Thirty per cent of those who went to
Britain had a third-level qualification and almost two-thirds had a
leaving certificate in secondary education. The corresponding
figure for males with leaving certificates was thirty-seven per cent.
Forty-three per cent of the 317 female emigrants who went to
destinations other than Britain had a third-level qualification and
many of these were in the 'emigrant aristocracy'.

Evidence also suggests that Irish women who belong to the
emigrant aristocracy in mainland Europe do not generally find
employment at the same level as their peers in the countries where
they settle. Thus MacÉinrí's Paris survey found that seventy-three
per cent of Irish women emigrants were working as teachers,
nurses or au pairs.[129] Things were not all that different in London,
where young Irish women are still among the best educated in the

city but are often not able to find employment commensurate with their education and qualifications. At first sight it may appear that female emigrants, given their strong representation in lower-middle class job ghettoes like secretarial work, nursing, teaching and banking, are better placed than their male counterparts. These four occupational categories alone accounted for just under fifty per cent of all female emigrants in the West of Ireland Survey. However, when wage levels in these occupations are compared to those in construction and related industries, it could be argued that, from a purely financial point of view, males are often still better off than female emigrants. (This does not mean that they fare better than women in terms of job security, working conditions and holiday allowances). Despite the 'gentrified' image of the successful 'career emigrant', the findings of most recent surveys support Hazelkorn's contention that most young Irish women are still holding jobs in the traditional job ghettoes of Irish emigrants.[130] Early marriage was traditionally regarded as the way out of the monotony and insecurity of life in these job ghettoes but this is no longer true today, and many young Irish women may be drifting from one casual job to another as part of their emigrant experience. This is particularly true of young women from rural and working-class backgrounds, many of whom never make it into the emigrant aristocracy. These are among the most hidden and most invisible members of Irish immigrant communities.

CONCLUSION

This study has focused on a neglected aspect of Irish emigration by emphasising Ireland's status as an emigrant nursery and a major supplier of skilled, unskilled and professional workers. Ireland's integration into the world economy from the late-eighteenth century onwards transformed large tracts of the country from areas of labour-intensive arable farming into heartlands of commercial agriculture. These were geared to the production of beef cattle and dairy produce for the export market and this caused profound social dislocations and contributed to large scale emigration. The transition from peasant agriculture and arable farming to rural capitalism probably occurred earlier in the midlands and south-east than it did in the west of Ireland. Wherever it occurred, it involved a remapping of the rural population of Ireland as people made room for farm machinery and cattle production throughout the nineteenth century. Unlike nineteenth-century Norway, for example, where emigration to the United States transformed peasants into small farmers, the rural exodus from Ireland more often than not resulted in the proletarianisation of the sons and daughters of the rural poor in the urban centres of the US and the UK.[131] The situation in late-nineteenth century France, where the modernisation of rural society transformed peasants into *Frenchmen* and *Frenchwomen*, was also unlike Ireland, where rural modern-isation transformed entire sections of rural society, and not only the rural poor, into emigrants.[132] Indeed the 'nationalisation' of rural Ireland under bourgeois nationalist hegemony was predicated upon the widespread emigration of her sons and daughters right up to the twentieth century. By the turn of the century capitalist relations of production hastened the disintegration of rural communities all over Ireland and reduced them to the status of 'emigrant nurseries'. These areas still retain the status of 'emigrant nurseries' today.

The post-war period not only underlined the extent of Ireland's dependence on Britain as a major host to Irish emigrants, it also witnessed a gradual gentrification and sanitisation of Irish emigration as Irish attitudes to emigration altered significantly. Emigration since the '60s has generally been explained away in terms of the peripheral location of Ireland or attributed to the social psychological attributes and aspirations of Irish young adults.

CONCLUSION

This study has focused on the structural roots of Irish emigration and shown that most emigration is not a voluntary activity attracting upwardly mobile individuals. It is instead a social class response to structural changes in the Irish economy, including changing relationships between Irish and overseas labour markets. Most young Irish emigrants are still going to England where they occupy the traditional job ghettoes of the Irish immigrant. Despite the undoubted existence of a new 'emigrant aristocracy', this is scarcely significant enough to talk of the 'gentrification' of Irish emigration.

This study has also shown that a world-systems approach to Irish emigration has a number of advantages over conventional explanations of Irish emigration, particularly those couched in the logic of modernisation theory and behaviouralism. Firstly, it avoids the pitfalls of national exceptionalism and cultural reductionism which over-emphasise the peculiar disposition of the Irish to emigrate to the neglect of comparative aspects of Irish emigration. Secondly, it allows us to see Irish emigration for what it was – a social process which linked core formation abroad with rural peripheralisation at home. However, far from being caused by the adventurous spirit of individualistic young adults, Irish emigration has always been a social response to restructuring processes operating at the level of the national and global economy. Thirdly, world-systems theory shows that far from being untouched by the forces of industrialisation, Irish labour occupied a central position in the international division of labour. Workers from Ireland have been crucial in the formation and maintenance of the core areas of the world economy. Except for short periods when emigration was halted by war, reversed by short-term upswings in the Irish economy, or curtailed by downturns in the British economy, this country has still functioned as a major supplier of labour in the world economy. This has meant that Irish labour, including young teenagers and female emigrants, has been this country's most consistent export and most mobile and neglected resource.

APPENDICES

Appendix 1: Occupational structure of male emigrants.

Occupation	Number Employed	% of total
Construction	462	39.7
Barwork	50	4.3
Mechanic	26	2.2
Factory Work	23	2.0
Cook	22	1.9
Shopwork	19	1.6
Lorry driver	18	1.5
Farm labourer	15	1.3
Security	13	1.1
Hotel work	12	1.0
Soldier	10	0.9
Caretaker	7	0.6
Stablehand	4	0.3
Taxi driver	2	0.2
Jockey	2	0.2
Childminder	1	0.09
Footballer	1	0.09
Cyclist	1	0.09
Lumberjack	1	0.9
Unemployed	21	1.8
Sub totals	710	60.9
Computer related	41	3.5
Student	36	3.1
Clerical	32	2.7
Salesman	30	2.6
Electrician	28	2.4
Bank Service	21	1.8
Teacher	18	1.5
British Telecom	11	0.9
Technician	10	0.9
Nursing	6	0.5

(appendix 1 cont'd)

Occupation	Number Employed	% of total
Social work	3	0.3
Musician	2	0.2
Librarian	1	0.09
Photographer	1	0.09
Sub totals	240	20.6
Engineer	73	6.3
Managerial	51	4.4
Dentist	11	0.9
Accountant	10	0.9
Doctor	9	0.8
Draughtsperson	9	0.8
Architect	6	0.5
Surveyor	5	0.4
Chemist	4	0.3
Pilot	3	0.3
Lawyer	3	0.3
Veterinary Surgeon	3	0.3
Publisher	1	0.09
Journalist	1	0.09
Geologist	1	0.09
Priest	1	0.09
Sub totals	191	16.4
Don't know	24	2.1
Total	**1,165**	**100%**

Source: West of Ireland Survey.

Appendix 2: Occupational structure of female emigrants.

Occupation	Number Employed	% of total
Shop Assistant	93	9.1
Waitress	71	6.9
Childcare	46	4.5
Housewife	37	3.6
Factory work	28	2.7
Barwork	25	2.4
Cook	12	1.2
Hairdresser	9	0.9
Horticulture	1	0.1
Unemployed	11	1.1
Sub-totals	333	32.5
Secretarial	204	20.0
Nursing	191	18.6
Teaching	61	5.9
Student	37	3.6
Financial Service	29	2.8
Bank Service	28	2.7
Technician	18	1.8
Computer-related	16	1.6
Air Hostess	8	0.8
Telecommunications	5	0.5
Social work	4	0.4
Police	3	0.3
Librarian	3	0.3
Journalist	1	0.1
Sub totals	608	59.2
Engineer	14	1.4
Managerial	13	1.3
Designer	6	0.6
Pharmacist	6	0.6
Doctor	5	0.5
Scientist	5	0.5
Dentist	5	0.5

(appendix 2 cont'd)

Occupation	Number Employed	% of total
Draughtsperson	4	0.4
Accountant	3	0.3
Lawyer	2	0.2
Radiographer	2	0.2
Geologist	1	0.1
Sub totals	66	6.4
Don't know	20	1.9
Totals	1,027	100%

Source: West of Ireland Survey.

REFERENCES

1. Kenneth H. Connell, *The Population of Ireland, 1756–1845* (Oxford: Oxford University Press, 1950); Damian Hannan, *Rural Exodus: A Study of the Forces Influencing the Large-scale Migration of Irish Youth* (London: Chapman, 1970); M. Goldring, *Faith of Our Fathers* (Dublin: Gill & Macmillan, 1982); James H. Johnson, 'Harvest migration from nineteenth-century Ireland', *Transactions and Papers, Institute of British Geographers*, vol. xli, 1967; and 'The two Irelands at the beginning of the nineteenth century' in Nigel Stephen and Robert E. Glascock (eds.), *Irish Geographical Studies in Honour of Estyn Evans* (Belfast: Blackstaff Press, 1970); Jan Mokyr, *Why Ireland Starved* (Oxford: Oxford University Press, 1985); P. Vaughan and D. Fitzpatrick, *Irish Historical Statistics* (Dublin: Gill & Macmillan, 1978).

2. F. S. L. Lyons, *Ireland Since the Famine* (London: Fontana, 1982), p. 44.

3. Karl Bottigheimer, *English Money and Irish Land* (Oxford: Oxford University Press 1971).

4. Kirby A. Miller, *Emigrants and Exiles* (New York: Oxford University Press, 1971).

5. M. A. Jones, *Destination America* (London: Weidenfeld and Nicolson, 1976), p. 17.

6. Miller, *Emigrants and Exiles*, p. 3.

7. B. Davidson, *The African Slave Trade* (New York: Little Brown, 1980), p. 60.

8. Jim Mac Laughlin, 'Industrial Capitalism, Unionism and Orangeism – an historical reappraisal', *Antipode*, vol. 12. no. 1, 1979.

9. Miller, *Emigrants and Exiles*.

10. Karl Marx, *Capital* (Moscow: Progress Press, 1976); Karl Marx and Friedrich Engles, *Selected Works*, vol. 1 (Moscow: Progress Press 1976).

References

11. Jim Mac Laughlin, 'Social characteristics and destinations of recent emigrants from selected regions in the west of Ireland', *Geoforum*, vol. 22, no. 3, 1991, p. 323.

12. Marx, *Capital*, p. 288.

13. A. Gramsci, *Selections from the Prison Notebooks* (London: Lawrence and Wishart, 1971), pp. 124–26.

14. Jim Mac Laughlin and J. A. Agnew, 'Hegemony and the regional question', *Annals of the Association of American Geographers*, vol. 76, no. 2, 1986.

15. Michael Higgins and John Gibbons, 'Shopkeeper-graziers and land agitation in Ireland, 1895–1900', in P. Drudy (ed.), *Irish Studies* (Cambridge: Cambridge University Press, 1982), pp. 77–92.

16. Miller, *Emigrants and Exiles*, p. 424.

17. David Fitzpatrick, *Irish Emigration, 1801–1921* (Dundalgan: Dundalgan Press, 1984); Prionnsias Breathnach, 'Uneven development and capitalist peripheralisation: the case of Ireland', *Antipode*, vol. 20, no. 2, 1988, pp. 122–41.

18. Prionnsias Breathnach, 'Uneven development and capitalist peripheralisation', p. 130.

19. K. Thedore Hoppen, *Elections, Politics and Society in Ireland, 1832–85* (Oxford: Oxford University Press, 1985).

20. Lyons, *Ireland Since the Famine*, p. 45.

21. Fitzpatrick, *Irish Emigration, 1801–1921*, p. 7.

22. Ibid., p. 9.

23. Cormac Ó Gráda, 'Seasonal migration and post-Famine adjustment in the west of Ireland', *Studia Hibernia*, vol. xxxiii, 1973 p. 56.

24. James E. Handley, *The Irish in Modern Scotland* (Cork: Cork University Press, 1947), p. 213.

25. Ó Gráda, 'Seasonal migration and post-Famine adjustment in the west of Ireland'.

26. David Fitzpatrick, 'A curious middle place: the Irish in Britain, 1871–1921', in Richard Swift and Stephen Gilley (eds.), *The Irish in Britain* (London: Barnes and Noble, 1989), p. 19.

27. S. H. Brandes, *Migration, Kinship and Community: Tradition and Transition in a Spanish Village* (New York: Academic Press, 1975).

28. C. H. Oldham, 'The incidence of emigration on town and country life in Ireland', *Journal of Social and Statistical Enquiry Society of Ireland*, vol. xiii, 1914, p. 213.

29. Robert D. C. Black, *Economic Thought and the Irish Question, 1817–1870* (Cambridge: Cambridge University Press, 1960); T. H. Boylan and T. P. Foley, *Political Economy and Colonial Ireland* (London: Routledge, 1992).

30. Hansard 1883, quoted in Miller, *Emigrants and Exiles*, p. 257.

31. George Dangerfield, *The Damnable Question: a Study in Anglo-Irish Relations* (London: Quartet, 1979), p. 17.

32. J. H. Tukes, *Donegal: Suggestions for Improvement of Congested Districts and Extension of Railways, Fisheries &c* (London: Ridgeway, 1889), p. 44.

33. Mary Lennon, M. McAdam and J. O' Brien, *Across the Water* (London: Virago, 1988), p. 22.

34. Gerard R. C. Keep, 'Official opinion on Irish emigration in the later-nineteenth century', *Irish Ecclesiastical Record,* vol. lxxxi, p. 417.

35. Boylan and Foley, *Political Economy and Colonial Ireland.*

36. Clive Dewey, 'Celtic agrarian legislation and the Celtic revival', *Past and Present,* vol. xxii, no. 3, 1978, pp. 32–35.

37. Keep, 'Official opinion on Irish emigration in the later-nineteenth century', p. 419.

38. Miller, *Emigrants and Exiles,* p. 458.

39. Brendan M. Kerr, 'Irish seasonal migration to Britain, 1800–1838, *Irish Historical Studies,* vol. 3, 1943, p. 372.

REFERENCES

40. Keep, 'Official opinion on Irish emigration in the later-nineteenth century', p. 445.

41. Ibid., p. 457.

42. Ibid., p. 418.

43. P. Commins, 'Rural social change', P. Clancy (ed.) *Ireland: A Sociological Profile* (Dublin: IPA and SAI Publications, 1988), p. 51.

44. Ibid., pp. 52–53.

45. S. Glynn, 'Irish immigration to Britain, 1911–1951', *Irish Economic and Social History,* vol. viii, 1981, p. 50.

46. E. Hazelkorn, 'British labour and Irish capital', *Galway Labour History Publication, The Emigrant Experience,* 1990, p. 125.

47. Lennon et al., *Across the Water,* pp. 24–25.

48. Carol Coulter, *Ireland: Between the First and Third Worlds* (Dublin: Attic Press, 1994) p. 96.

49. Breathnach, 'Uneven development and capitalist peripheralisation'.

50. Raymond Crotty, *Ireland in Crisis* (Dingle: Brandon, 1986), pp. 84–85.

51. Ibid., p. 85.

52. Breathnach, 'Uneven development and capitalist peripheralisation', p. 136.

53. Ibid.; Wickham 'The politics of dependent capitalism: international capital and the nation-state,' Andrew Morgan and Bill Purdie (eds.), *Ireland: Divided Nation, Divided Class* (London: Macmillan, 1980).

54. P. Murray and James Wickham, 'Technocratic ideology and the reproduction of inequality: the case of the electronics industry in the Republic of Ireland', G. Day et al. (eds.), *Diversity and Decomposition in the Labour Market* (London: Gower, 1982), p. 204.

55. Ethel Crowley, 'Factory Girls: the implication of multinational investment for female employment in the Republic of Ireland', *Occasional Papers in Social Science,* (Belfast: Queen's University, 1993).

56. James Wickham, 'The politics of dependent capitalism' p. 204.

57. John A. Kennedy, *The Irish in Britain* (London: Routledge and Kegan Paul, 1973).

58. Eoin O'Malley, 'The problem of late industrialisation and the experience of the Republic of Ireland', *Cambridge Journal of Economics,* vol. 9, pp. 246–62.

59. Raymond Crotty, *Irish Agricultural Production* (Cork: Cork University Press, 1966); J.G. Hughes and Brendan Walsh, 'Migration flows between Ireland, the UK and the rest of the world', *European Demographic Review,* vol. 7, no. 4, pp. 125–49; Joseph Lee, *Ireland 1912–1985* (Cambridge: Cambridge University Press, 1990); Lyons, *Ireland Since the Famine;* Brendan Walsh, 'Emigration: some policy issues', *Irish Banking Review,* vol. 2, pp. 3–13.

60. Miller, *Emigrants and Exiles,* pp. 6–7.

61. Ibid., p. 556.

62. David Lloyd, 'Making sense of the dispersal', *The Irish Reporter,* vol. 13, p. 4.

63. Ibid., p. 4.

64. Mary Holland, 'A reluctance to examine what nationalism really means to us', *The Irish Times,* 26 August, 1993.

65. David Harvey, *The Condition of Postmodernity* (London: Blackwell, 1992).

66. Z. Mlinar, 'Individuation and globalization: the transformation of territorial organization', Z. Mlinar (ed.), *Globalization and Territorial Identities* (Aldershot: Avebury, 1992), p. 26.

67. Etienne Balibar, 'Es Gibt Keinen Staat in Europa: racism and politics in Europe today', *New Left Review,* vol. 186, 1991, p. 14.

68. Fintan O'Toole, 'Permanence and tradition are illusions in a makeshift society,' *The Irish Times,* 30 May, 1994.

69. Fintan O'Toole, *A Mass for Jesse James* (Dublin: New Island Books, 1990),

70. Quoted in D. Massey, 'A place called home', *New Formations,* no. 17, 1992, p. 15.

71. O'Toole, *A Mass for Jesse James*, p. 125.

72. Ibid., p. 122.

73. Ibid., p. 124.

74. John Waters, 'Exploding the modern myth of backward Ireland', *The Irish Times,* 13 April, 1993.

75. Kevin Whelan, 'The bases of regionalism' in Prionnsias O'Driscoll (ed.), *Culture in Ireland, Regions and Identity* (Belfast: Institute of Irish Studies, 1993), p. 19.

76. Ibid., p. 15.

77. E. Cobbe and S. MacCárthaigh (eds.), *Living and Working in Europe* (Dublin: Gill & Macmillan, n.d.), p. xv.

78. Joseph Lee, 'Ireland today – poor performance from a talented people?' *The Irish Times,* 13 January, 1990.

79. Jim Mac Laughlin, '"Mother Ireland's" multinational families', *The Irish Reporter,* vol. 15, 1994, pp. 12–16.

80. Tom Whelan, 'The new emigrants', *Newsweek,* 10 October, 1987.

81. Ibid.

82. *The Irish Times,* 13 October, 1987.

83. Robert Foster, 'Young emigrants still looking west', *The Irish Times,* 14 April, 1987.

84. Gearóid Ó Tuathaigh, 'The historical pattern of Irish emigration: some labour aspects', *Galway Labour History Group Publication, The Emigrant Experience,* 1991, p. 24.

85. John A. Agnew, 'The devaluation of place in social science', Agnew and James (eds.), *The Power of Place* (Boston: Unwin, 1989), pp. 17–45.

86. Hassan Hakimian, *Labour Transfers and Economic Development: Theoretical Perspectives and Case Studies from Iran* (New York: Wheatsheaf, 1990).

87. Karl Mannheim, *Ideology and Utopia* (New York, Harcourt, Brace and World, 1936).

88. Peter Taylor, *Political Geography: World Economy, Nation-State and Locality* (London: Longman, 1985), p. 16.

89. Ó Tuathaigh, 'The historical pattern of Irish emigration: some labour aspects', p. 16.

90. Ibid., p. 16.

91. Damian Courtney, *Recent Trends in Emigration from Ireland* (Cork: Department of Social Science, RTC, 1989).

92. Deaglán de Breadún, 'Three hundred have gone from Lettermore in a year', *The Irish Times,* 3 February, 1986.

93. Courtney, *Recent Trends in Emigration from Ireland.*

94. Anthony Cronin, 'The law that keeps the huddled masses out', *The Irish Times,* 15 January, 1988.

95. M. Corcoran, 'Infomalization of metropolitan labour forces: the case of Irish immigrants in the New York construction industry', *Irish Journal of Sociology,* vol. 1, 1991, pp. 31–51.

96. O'Toole, *The Irish Times*, 30 May, 1994.

97. De Breadún, *The Irish Times,* 3 February, 1986.

98. Mark T. Brennock, 'A time of bitter-sweet reunions for young emigrants', *The Irish Times,* 21 December, 1988.

99. Courtney, *Recent Trends in Emigration from Ireland,* p. 11.

100. NESC Report, 1991.

101. John Lovering, 'Postmodernism, Marxism and locality research', *Antipode,* vol. 21, 1984, pp. 11–14.

102. Elizabeth M. Thomas-Hope, 'Caribbean skilled international migration and the transnational household', *Geoforum,* vol. 19, no. 4, 1988, pp. 423–32.

103. Russell King and Ian Shuttleworth, 'Ireland's new wave emigration in the 1980s', *Irish Geography,* vol. 21, 1988, pp. 104–08.

104. J. J. Sexton, 'Recent changes in Irish population and in the pattern of emigration', *Irish Banking Review,* vol. 3, 1987, pp. 31–44.

105. De Breadún, *The Irish Times,* 3 February, 1986.

106. Ó Tuathaigh, 'The historical pattern of Irish emigration', p. 23.

107. F. H. Aalen and H. Brody, *Gola: Life and Last Days of an Island Community* (Cork: Mercier, 1969); H. Brody, *Inishkillane* (London: Allen Lane, 1973).

108. B. Anderson, *Imagined Communities* (London: Verso, 1983).

109. Mac Laughlin, '"Mother Ireland's" multinational families', p. 6.

110. Brandes, *Migration, Kinship and Community*.

111. Aalen and Brody: *Gola: Life and Last Days of an Island Community*; John Healy, *No One Shouted Stop* (Achill: Healy House, 1988), p. 28; T. Steel, *The Death of St Kilda* (London: Fontana, 1988), p. 16.

112. De Breadún, *The Irish Times,* 3 February 1986.

113. Bronwen Walter, *Irish Women in London* (London: Spider Press, 1989).

114. K. Kelly and T. Nic Giolla Choille, *Emigration Matters for Women* (Dublin: Attic Press, 1990), p. 21.

115. Piaras MacÉinrí, 'The new Europeans: the Irish in Paris today', D. Keogh and J. Mullholland (eds.), *Emigration, Employment and Enterprise* (Cork: Hibernian University Press, 1989).

116. King and Shuttleworth, 'Ireland's new wave emigration'.

117. Walter, *Irish Women in London*.

118. *The Irish Times,* 13 July, 1988.

119. D. MacAmhlaigh, *The Irish Navvy* (London: Macmillan, 1967).

120. Lennon et al., *Across the Water;* J. Rudd, 'The emigration of Irish women', *Irish Studies,* vol. 9, no. 3, pp. 3–11.

121. P. Meenan, *The Irish Economy Since 1922* (Liverpool: Liverpool University Press, 1970).

122. P. Scheper-Hughes, *Saints, Scholars and Schizophrenics* (Berkeley: University of California Press, 1979).

123. Hasia Diner, *Erin's Daughters in America* (Baltimore: Johns Hopkins University Press, 1983); J. Rudd, 'The emigration of Irish women', *Irish Studies*, vol. 9, no. 3, 1987, pp. 3–11.

124. Kelly and Nic Giolla Choille, *Emigration Matters for Women*, p. 17.

125. Ibid., p. 16.

126. Ibid., p. 21.

127. B. Walter, *Irish Women in London* (London: Spider Press, 1989), p. 34.

128. Kelly and Nic Giolla Choille, p. 13.

129. MacÉinrí, 'The new Europeans: the Irish in Paris today', p. 15.

130. Hazelkorn, 'British Labour and Irish Capital'.

131. J. Gjerde, *From Peasants to Farmers: the migration from Balestrand, Norway, to the Upper Middle West* (Cambridge: Cambridge University Press, 1985).

132. Eugen Weber, *Peasants into Frenchmen: the Modernization of Rural France* (Stanford: Stanford University Press, 1976).